MW01101632

Consequence

Beyond Resisting Rape

by
Loolwa Khazzoom

Pearl in a Million Press

Copyright ©2001
Loolwa Khazzoom

All rights reserved. No part of this book may be reproduced in any form, except for inclusion of brief quotations in a review, without permission in writing from the author or publisher.

Library of Congress Control Number: 00-91250

Additional copies of this book are available by mail. Send $15 (includes tax and postage) to

Pearl in a Million Press
2425-B Channing Way, Suite 203
Berkeley, CA 94704
510-595-4642

Published in the United States by
Pearl in a Million Press
2425-B Channing Way, Suite 203
Berkeley, CA 94704
510-595-4642

Printed in the United States by
Morris Publishing
3212 East Highway 30
Kearney, NE 68847
1-800-650-7888

CONSEQUENCE IN CYBERSPACE
www.loolwa.com/consequence.html

for girls who don't take shit
for boys who love us

cover art:

Margarita Alcantara-Tan

www.bamboogirl.com
bamboogirl@bamboogirl.com

Table of Contents

II. From Here On Out

Preface

I write this book as a woman who believes that revolution is imperative and that it starts within each of us and our private lives. I draw from my own life's experiences of violence, and from my battles against this violence, in the many forms and degrees it has permeated my life. I draw from time spent observing women and men interacting; time spent experimenting with gender roles; and time spent directly challenging men on their behavior towards women. I draw from years of feminist conferences, marches, rallies, actions, and self-defense training and from years of speaking with women late into the night about how violence has affected us all.

In this book, I address race, ethnicity, class, sexual orientation, and religion as each of these identities directly or indirectly have touched my own life's experiences. I acknowledge there are numerous additional ways these identities can shape one's experiences as a woman.

Throughout the social critiques in this book, I refer to "men" and "male behavior." In doing so, I address the patriarchal power structure and the behavior of the overwhelming majority of men in this society. I acknowledge and honor that there also are men who struggle alongside women in vigilantly fighting patriarchy. There simply need to be more – *much* more.

The bulk of experiences I recount in this book took place in Israel, but the harassment scenarios I describe are not an *Israeli* phenomenon. Equivalent or worse kinds of assaults have happened to me (and countless other women) all over the world. Quite simply, Israel always has been a place of spiritual transformation for me. The country yet again played this role in my life, as I took new steps in fighting violence against women.

Dedication

This book is dedicated to all the women imprisoned for fighting to live; to all the "witches" burned for living independently; to all the girls punished for demanding dignity; to all the females who risked, despite all the odds and the fears; to our Creator for giving us the courage to dare; to the warriors on whose shoulders we stand; to all the friends who love and support us; and to our future society, intolerant of violence against women.

Honors

In recognition of Judie, who believed in me when I did not believe in myself; EJ, who lent me the financial support to pursue my dreams; and Joanne Stewart and Lee Ann Torlakson, for teaching me everything I know about writing.

Pushing the Envelopes:

New Responses to Old Behaviors

Feminism at the Falafel Stand

"Hello, sweetie, how are you?"

It started from the moment I stepped off the airport bus. Innocuous-sounding enough, but poison in its context. Wherever I went, whatever I did, there he would be, in my face. Asking me questions, making comments. I could not lie on the beach alone, walk down the street alone, sit at a cafe alone. It was constant, unceasing, without mercy. *And without consequence.*

"Don't start with me," I cautioned the first two. "Whopa!" they said, simultaneously impressed and entertained by my response. They left me alone after that; but usually I was not so lucky.

Cute young men, creepy old men, and everything in-between. They saw female flesh and went for it: "Hello, how are you today?"

"I want to be alone," I replied. He kept coming towards me, still talking. "I said I want to be alone." He did not stop. "Get the fuck away from me! I don't want to talk with you, and I don't want you near me!" He called *me* crazy. He started prancing about, yelling about what a nut I was. I moved to a different part of the beach. *I* moved.

"Hello, sweetie..." The jogger talked at me as he ran by. He ran past me again, talking again. He stopped and came over to me. I tried the ignoring technique. It didn't work. "Can't you just leave a woman alone? Can you deal with the concept that I don't want to talk with you? I am really sick of this! Get away from me!"

I had been thinking for a long time about the idea of hitting men who harassed me. The prospect was looking quite delicious at this point. I was close, very close...

"Hello, how are you?" I was lying on the wide low wall bracing the stairs down, listening to music on my walkman. The sun was shining on me, and I was feeling good. The idiot kept talking. I opened my eyes a slit to see who he was. His face was temptingly close to my foot. I considered the possibilities. The moron kept talking. "Hello?! Hellooooooo?!" he said, waving a hand back and forth, as if to wake me up. I jumped up and verbally devoured him. "I'm not answering you because I don't want to talk with you! Get the fuck out of here!" I was right in his face. He freaked out and retreated, whimpering. I wished I had kicked him. *I was getting closer.*

I arrived at the Jerusalem bus stop, to meet a friend for lunch. We chose a tasty falafel/shwarma restaurant halfway down the block. I placed my order and looked around, only to see one of the two young soldiers near me staring at my chest. I pretended it was not happening and tried distracting myself. I went over to look at the wall-to-wall pictures of Mizrahi rabbis. How often, after all, did I have the pleasure of seeing pictures of non-Ashkenazi rabbis, even in restaurants owned by Mizrahim?[1]

"Are you from England?" the soldier asked when I returned, still staring at my chest. "What are you looking at?" I challenged. "He's looking at your backpack," his friend answered. As I struggled to think of what to say next, the friend added, "He's staring at your breasts." "What are you, chauvinists?" I replied. Damn! Just didn't sound as good in Hebrew. No punch. "G-d forbid!" the friend said in mock offense. They giggled with delight, thoroughly amused by themselves.

"Why?" the friend continued, "is it a sin for a guy to look?" I practically jumped up his nostrils, shouting at him. "Yes, it's disgusting. Women are not slabs of meat for men to gape at." I had an idea. "How would you feel if women talked to you while staring at your dick?" I leaned over sideways in front of the guy, placing my head squarely in front of his penis. "Would you like it if women talked to you this way?" They both laughed, in a way that was partly disconcerted and partly amused. "Oh, you think it's funny?" I asked. There was no stopping me now. "What about if I hit it?"
I slammed my hand under his penis.

He jumped back, startled, confused. A woman started running around in circles, yelling, "What is it? What's happening? What's going on?" The man behind the counter calmly kept making my falafel. "See," I shouted at the soldier I just hit, "that's what it feels like when men stare at my chest. It feels as violating as being hit." By this point, the guy who originally stared at my chest had run out of the store. I ran after him. I was on a roll. I found him outside, laughing uncontrollably, with his penis partially erect. "Oh, you think it's funny?" I asked. "What about if I hit *yours?*" I slammed my hand under his penis, grabbing his balls. He stopped laughing. I gave him the same speech.

I ran back in the store, yelling god knows what. "Hey," I said to the soldier inside, "You've got a cute butt!" *Slam!* I hit it. The soldier outside came back in. "In fact, you've got a cute butt too!" *Slam!* This guy was really upset by now, shifting back and forth, unsure what the hell to do. I was ready to take him on. He just stood there shifting on his feet, looking thoroughly distressed. I was having a blast.

The man behind the counter finished making my falafel. The woman still was running around frantically, trying to figure out what was going on. I paid for my falafel and thanked the man, beaming with delight. I walked out of the restaurant, laughing with my head thrown back. Deep, unbridled laughter from my belly. Chortles of freedom and power. It was one of the greatest moments of my life, and I was in absolute ecstasy.

These guys thought they could get away with speaking to and looking at me however they pleased, regardless of how I felt or what I said. Our interaction occurred in a social context where women usually do not confront verbal or visual assault - or physical assault, for that matter. We usually look away; try to ignore the men; pretend that what is happening is not actually happening; or become brain dead and giggly, deluding ourselves that the men actually are flattering us. At best, we tell the guys to leave us alone; or in more colorful terms, we tell them to fuck off.

So what.

There is barely any significant consequence to male assault of women. Men can and do assault women in various forms, with absolutely no physical, economic, political, or emotional ramifications whatsoever. In fact, men can gain more power[2] by assaulting women than by refraining from assault. By verbally assaulting women in the street, they can score points with their pals. By raping women in a fraternity, they can score points in the old boys' network. Considering the patriarchal social context where women are used as mere instruments for male existence, assaulting women is all part of the game plan; and there is far more *incentive* to assault than there is *deterrent*.

Given these factors, women's verbal resistance is all part of the power trip: *You can say no, and I will continue anyhow. You have no power whatsoever, girly girl. You have no impact. I, to the contrary, clearly DO.* For this reason, the soldiers got even more delight out of our interaction when I verbally resisted their assault. How titillating; she's so cute when she's angry! And look - we can keep assaulting her, and nothing will happen to us!

Or so they thought...

A number of women think it is a big deal and strong enough to verbally resist male visual/verbal assault. I propose that to see it as such is to operate from a place where we perceive the men as being above us, stronger than us, like parent or some other "authority" figures; and to perceive ourselves as children, underneath them, *so that it takes tremendous courage for us just to say anything at all.*

Saying something - anything - is perhaps better than not resisting at all. But let's go beyond the bare minimum already. Let's do something that has *impact, consequence;* something that will *deter* assault, something that will turn the assaultive energy around - in the heat of the moment - and *give* us power instead of *taking* it from us. Let's go beyond merely *resisting* what they are doing to us; let's start *doing* something to them...

Assault against women happens every day, every hour, every minute, every second, multiple times a day in every woman's life, in many different forms. *None of this assault should be happening, period.* And I think it is time to stop it, whatever it takes.

In Search of Security

At the fancy hotel bordering the Eilat Youth Hostel, a Moroccan-Israeli wedding party was taking place by the pool; and my Dutch roommate and I went to check it out. After about an hour, she went back to sleep; but I stayed. I continued dancing to the Mizrahi music, elated by this rare opportunity to be surrounded by my culture. Finally, the party started dying down, and I left.

When I reached the landing of the youth hostel, however, the music started up again. By this point, it was 1:00 AM, and there was no one around. I started dancing on the landing, having a blast. I felt more free than I had since arriving. I am characteristically uninhibited, but I had stopped acting as my authentic self. I no longer could stand the constant male attention assaulting my space.

A couple passed by me, smiling appreciatively and supportively, without saying anything to disturb me. "Now this is *good* attention," I thought to myself. "This is the kind of attention that is life-affirming, that connects - not violates - people."

Good attention is where I am walking down the street, and someone looks me in the eye and smiles brightly, in appreciation of my beauty. Good attention is where I am sitting alone, and someone approaches me, asking with sincerity, "Would you like some company?" Good attention is where I am dancing in the surf, and someone watches me quietly from the beach. Good attention, in other words, is where someone honors *me* - a spirit independent of the individual giving me attention; a person with her own will, her own mass, and her own agenda; one who is entitled to the body space around her.

Bad attention, to the contrary, is where I am walking down the street, and someone looks up and down my body

with the assessment-of-inventory look, saying, "Hey, baby..."
Bad attention is where I am sitting alone; someone sits next to
me without asking if I want company; and when I say I want to
be alone, the person stays. Bad attention is where I am
dancing in the surf, and someone runs down towards me,
whistling, clapping, and talking at me incessantly. Bad
attention, in other words, is where someone meets [his]
own needs at my expense, using my being as a means to [his]
own fulfillment.

I live my life the way I live it because I am who I am. I
do not live or act *for* other people. If anything, I am who I am
despite all the attempts to squash me out. The overwhelming
amount of male heterosexual attention nonetheless comes from
the perspective that as a woman, I am going through the world
solely for the benefit of men - as if my body exists for their
eyes; as if my joy exists for their consumption; as if my
achievements exist for their ownership. In this light, *I find that
what passes for complimentary attention is often assaultive
attention*, more about a power trip than about admiration.

To truly honor another person, I feel, is to make oneself
vulnerable; for to approach someone with respect is to
recognize her/his autonomous power. As such, to *respectfully*
share our admiration of or desire to connect with somebody is
to risk not being admired or desired in return. To say, "May I
join you?" is to risk the answer, "No."

I believe that rejection is one of the most painful human
experiences, as I believe we all have deep, core desires to be
seen - to be recognized and appreciated for the glorious, unique
spirits we are. I believe that most men approach women in a
way that wraps up admiration in a coat of self-protection, so
they avoid risking the vulnerability that comes with respectful
treatment.[3] Rather than ask an attractive woman if she would
like his company, for example, a man will just sit next to her
and begin talking. On a more extreme level, rather than ask a
woman if she wants sex, he will just force it on her.

By approaching a woman in this dominating kind of
way, a man does not "allow" a woman the room to reject him.
Even if she does ultimately leave him, shoo him away, or fight
him off, he has managed to take something from her - namely,
her power to make simple choices about her own body and life,

at least without a fight. As such, the score may seem more "even" to the man, and he may come away feeling more power than if he simply asked and she simply rejected.

In this way, heterosexual male attention towards women is often more about power-over than about connection; more about violence than appreciation. It is about protecting male ego *at the expense of female autonomy,* where the "score" is far from even. A woman does not actually "take" from a man by rejecting him; she simply does not give him what he wants. In approaching a woman dominatingly, however, a man *does* take from a woman: He disrespects her will; he robs her of physical space; and he denies her the ability to make personal choices in peace.

Patriarchal societies throughout the world support and insulate this power dynamic. As girls, we are taught that our primary objective in life is to receive male attention, and we are taught that we are prudes or bitches (the ultimate insult?) if we reject it. We are taught that whistling and ogling are forms of flattery, and we are trained to rely desperately upon this "flattery" for our self-esteem. In effect, we are sculpted into pawns for a "win-win" power trip for men; so that men can approach us virtually risk-free, without emotional vulnerability and with almost a guarantee of "positive" female response.[4]

For a woman who even remotely is interested in male attention, I feel that male-female relations are, at best, a disaster - more about power wars than about any kind of connection. Even where there is potential for connection, the male-female dynamic can be so volatile and draining that a woman may not be or feel safe in trusting whatever potential she senses.

I grew up with more male friends than female friends, and in my teen years, I was "boy-crazy;" my friends had difficulty keeping up with my latest crush. As I came into my power, however, and as I began exploring sexually, I had so many experiences of male violence that I ended up retreating almost completely from any interactions with men. Currently, I have hardly any male friends; and most identify as "queer."

I used to love meeting gorgeous men. Now I barely bother looking at them. What would be the point? I do not have interest in or energy for any degree of violence in my life; I do not want my intimate relationships to be a constant struggle to breathe. As such, I hardly can imagine myself being passionately attracted to and involved with a man these days, given the oppression that goes on in heterosexual relationships. As one lesbian-by-choice put it while phasing out of being straight, "I've been down this path before; I've read this book already...Same old, same old, same old. Why bother?"

In fact, I barely bother talking to any men now, unless they already have gone through my friends' screening; or they are in my social circle and appear pro-feminist when we hang out in groups. Even then, I do not bring them into my home, unless they have proved themselves "safe" over time.

I hate it.

I hate the fact that I barely can trust a man when I'm asking directions. So many times, he will make a friendly comment; I will be friendly back; and he will look up and down my body like a predator, reminding me not to "fall" for a human connection the next time around. I hate the fact that I barely can look into the eyes of men I pass on the street; because they often turn our connected gaze into ogling me, or they *demand* conversation from me. I hate the fact that so many men have looked at me like a predator so many times; and so many men I trusted have violated my trust, that I cannot be exactly sure of the intent of bisexual and straight male friends, when their gaze drops down to the level of my chest.

It is like a death happening every time.

Men themselves lose out when approaching women in dominating ways: They do not get to experience how it feels to be welcomed by women, from women's places of *choice*. They do not get to share true *connection*, which exists only between full, autonomous human beings. They do not acquire true power; for they are so terrified of women's rejection - and thus are so *dependent* on women's approval - that they go out of their way to circumvent women's ability to dismiss them. And they do not get attention from many wonderful, beautiful women who are staying miles away from men, as a result of male dominance.

The irony of it all is that in trying to secure and insure a woman's embrace, a man may drive a woman irretrievably far away from him. In trying to deny her the room to reject him, he also may deny her the room to appreciate him.

The way things are now, if a woman has no *investment* in receiving male attention, she undermines the whole power setup where the man is guaranteed some kind of perceived "victory" over her. I believe many heterosexual men feel threatened by lesbianism for this reason alone, if not for a slew of additional reasons. It is no surprise that when women resist male verbal / visual assault, men frequently shout the refrain "fucking dyke" (not realizing they are shouting a compliment).

I have found that men not only expect acceptance of their behavior, but they expect *and feel entitled to* positive responses to it. Not only have men verbally / visually assaulted me through their initial approaches; but when I have not bowed to their wills and responded in the ways they desired, the men have become hostile, even physically threatening.

The swifter and more violent the responses to our simply claiming our own space, the more it is apparent how much power we actually *do* have. The more it is apparent how much the powers-that-currently-be are weaker than us and how much they are terrified of our finding out.

The Achilles heel of male dominance over women is that male[5] identity currently is defined in a way that *depends upon* women. Without women feeding male egos, submitting to male wills, and playing out male fantasies, what is left of patriarchy? Most men's lives revolve around dominating women. If women refuse to be dominated, there is nothing left of most men.

The joke on men is that by constructing their sense of power on a model of power-*over*, they inadvertently have placed women at the *center* of their power; which is why the faintest shade of female power is so threatening to men: The moment women realize and act upon our power in a unilateral way, male dominance over women will be *impossible*, and patriarchy will die. Just remember the level of national freak-out that occurred after one single woman, Lorena Bobbitt, made a tiny little stroke with her hand...

And now for the way not *to approach me...*

Suddenly, I was assaulted by the sound of five young men whistling, clapping, and hey-babying me from the landing above. *Oh, god,* I thought, *not again.* I had been feeling so good.

I was determined not to let them rain on my parade. I focused on myself, meditating towards a space where they did not exist, where it was just me and the music. I was doing pretty well, when one of the guys came down and started talking at me. He would not shut up.

I have heard a number of spiritually-oriented people talk about transcending bad energy that comes our way; and in that context, I have vague recollections of people telling me to "just go beyond" verbal assault, while in the face of it. Considering the fact that full-scale physical assault frequently begins with verbal assault that may seem harmless, it actually can be *dangerous* - as extreme as life-threatening - to dismiss the "verbiage" (verbal garbage) being thrown a woman's way.

I generally track what verbal assailants say to me and where they are in physical proximity to me, as a means of gauging the level of potential danger. In this case, I initially allowed myself the luxury of tuning the guys out, because they were a floor above me. I want to emphasize, however, that "just ignoring" or "going beyond" verbal assault is not an option most of the time. I truly wish it were. I would love to walk through the world in my own spiritual bubble, tuning out the various attention coming my way...

"Why don't you do your *own* dance instead of interfering with mine," I suggested. He came over to dance with me. I stopped him. "No, don't dance *with me.* Do your *own* dance." He tentatively twisted around a little, for about three seconds, laughing nervously the whole time. His pals above laughed nervously with him. "You see," I said. "You're just a coward. You're a little boy.[6] You don't have the courage I have. Don't bother me." I shooed him away, waving my hand at him dismissively. The loser went upstairs, defeated, and the boys left me alone.

For a few minutes.

"*Hey baby...*" The assault continued. Whistling, kissing sounds, the works. It would be pointless to tell them to leave me alone; they would use my resistance to further their predatory rush. They would view my protest as cute and entertaining, like the squeal of a furry little mouse trapped in glue. I had been through the scenario enough times to know. My words and anger would carry no weight. *No consequence -> no threat -> no power -> no impact.*

I leaned back against the banister, crossing my hands over my chest. "Come on," I said, "*I* want to see a show. Entertain *me.*" I began clapping. "Come on! Dance for me! Come on!" I whistled and hooted at them. They looked to each other with uncertainty, unsure what to do next, laughing nervously and shifting around. "I'm waaaaaiting," I cooed. One of them ventured four or five little steps, laughing self-consciously the whole time. It was pathetic.

I made dramatic gestures of disappointment. "You see? You're cowards. You bother me, but you're too afraid to dance yourself. You make all this noise, but you can't do anything. If you're not going to give me a show, leave me alone." I shooed them away dismissively. After hanging around momentarily, they retreated into the building.

I was on a high. I felt I finally figured out how to overcome this plague. I myself took on the observer role, making it impossible for them to sit and take from me. In a physical way, I refused to be a spectator sport. What more, I identified their spectatorship as cowardice and my freedom as power. As such, by using their own tactics against them, I managed to turn the tables around.

But minutes later, they were back with the same routine. It became clear that to *maintain* the "upper hand" in this kind of situation, I would have to play the observer role non-stop. I could not just do my thing in peace.

I tried out the role once more, hanging back with my arms crossed and demanding a show from my spectators. Not surprisingly, they gave another poor performance; so again, I shooed them away: "You're just little boys. You're cowards. If *you* can't dance yourself, don't go bothering *my* dancing. Just go away. Get out of here." They left.

Surprise, surprise, they were back again, clapping, whistling, etc., etc., etc. "Look, I've had it!" I shouted. "Just get the fuck away from me! Leave me alone! I am sick of this!" They left...

...and returned. I decided it was time to hit one of them. I had been wanting to try out something like this for a long time.

My plan was to get one of them downstairs and use him as an example. I wooed the asshole of choice, smiling and beckoning him with a motioning finger: "Come down here! I want to talk with you!" The dork got all excited. "Me?!" He ecstatically pointed a finger at himself, then turned and pointed at the guys on his right and left, questioning which one of them was the lucky one. *Oh, the irony of it all.* "YOU." I pointed intently at him. His pals began ribbing and slapping him with hearty congratulations, as he began his strut downstairs. I laughed heartily. Boy, was he in for a big surprise.

I was quite excited. I began doing stretches, warming down from dancing and warming up for slapping the asshole. I felt completely centered, grounded in my power. I smiled and laughed in anticipation.

When I stood up, one of the guys from upstairs was right in front of me, and it was not the one I had called down. He was the one guy who had not left the balcony at the times the others had. He mostly had stood in one place, staring a cold, fixed stare at me. He had bugged the shit out of me, more than all the others. There was nothing friendly about him. He had not responded to anything I had said. He had not so much as twitched when I had yelled at him to stop watching me and leave me alone.

So there he was, a few feet away, yet again staring fixedly at me. My expression changed abruptly from a smile to a snarl. I went right up to his face. "I want you to leave me alone!" I shouted. He didn't budge. "*What's the prob-*lem?" he sneered. "The problem is that you've been harassing me, and I want you to leave me alone!" I stepped even closer, practically breathing down his throat. "*What's the prob-*lem?" he sneered again. He was so smug in his security that nothing could happen to him, *that there would be no consequence for his actions...*

Crack! My fury raged into his face, as my hand slammed full force into his cheek. *The impact was LOUD.* **Snap!** That was his neck. **Whoooooooosh!** His head flew around, full speed, almost 180°.

Damn, that felt good.

I must say, that moment was one of the most powerful, satisfying, and wholly gratifying in my life. I mean **satisfying.** I never will forget the strength, rootedness, and pure, radiant glee that filled me, as I witnessed the play-by-play follow-through of choosing to raise my hand and give that fucker what he deserved. Ha, ha!

I did it. I finally did it.

How often have we stood there helplessly? How many times have we left a situation, giving *our* space over to assailants? How often have we said something, but our words have had no impact...or worse, how often have our words been used to escalate the assault against us?

We live in a social context where men's words and non-touching behavior can be *as violent* to women as various levels of physical assault: Given the backdrop of patriarchy - where countless men badger, rape, and murder countless women every day; where men systematically exclude women from access to power and privilege; where our senses are assaulted unceasingly with images of degraded women; and where men economically, physically, and institutionally punish women for speaking our minds, taking up our space, or resisting violence against us - there is an added weight to and power behind men's words and non-touching behavior, bolstering the impact of their actions.

When a man ogles a woman, for example, it is not an isolated incident. Chances are that hundreds or thousands of other men ogled her before. Chances are that men in fact ogled her so frequently and made her feel so violated that she stopped wearing the clothes she liked, fearing it "showed too much;" that she stopped standing as tall as she wanted, because doing so made her chest "too" prominent; that she stopped smiling or looking around as she walked, to avoid "attracting" attention; that she stopped taking that shortcut, going to that nightclub, or visiting that neighborhood; and that she gained 10 or more pounds to avoid being ogled anymore. Chances are that over time, she was *forced* to contort her life around the behavior of men, railroaded into a lifestyle that goes against her personality, will, desires, and natural body shape.

Mr. Y is not the only man ogling Ms. X; Ms. X is not the only woman men ogle; and ogling is not the only way men invade women's space. One man ogling one woman thus holds much more punch than the individual act alone. The act takes place in a world of a power imbalance, where women's bodies are bought and sold for and by men; where "wives" frequently are domestic and sexual slaves to men; where women earn two-thirds what men earn, for the same job...And on and on and on.

As such, a man does not need to say or do much to a woman to cause significant harm. With a few words, he can make her feel the weight of the entire patriarchal system bearing down on her, as if he physically is kicking her in the stomach - or worse, as if he literally is penetrating inside her. I personally have experienced the intensity of such physical sensations in my body during men's verbal/visual assaults. I also have witnessed countless women react *physically* to such assaults by hunching over or scrunching their bodies tightly, the same way many do when physically assaulted.

Women's words and non-touching behavior simply cannot have the same impact as men's. In a patriarchal reality, men speak and act *with the power of the system* and a history of violation behind their words and behaviors towards women. Women, however, carry no parallel threatening force behind us. (Yet.)

"Stop/Go away/Back off/Leave me alone/Cut it out/I mean it, get away from me..." And the assault continues. With words, looks, or touch. In most cases - especially on the street - there is no consequence for male violence against women; *and men know it.* They know that with the exception of extreme physical attack, *their violence will fall through the cracks of legal justice systems.*[7] I find it no accident that currently unpunishable male violence is both common and constant.

And as I will discuss later, I find it no accident that such forms of male violence are currently unpunishable.

Earlier in the evening, I had asked my Dutch roommate how she deals with this issue. She gave an example that when she goes to the beach, she tries to go where there are no men; and if men find her, she gets up and leaves. From many previous discussions with other women, I find that her approach is the most common. Garden-variety, socially-sanctioned male violence thus forces women into a subordinate, deferential, second-class reality, where women constantly have to work ourselves around men; where we have to contort ourselves to fit the tiny little slivers of space men may be so "gracious" as to leave for us.

I am sick of it.

After recovering, this idiot looked like he wanted to fight. He started hopping around like a moron, rolling up his sleeves. He jumped back and forth, back and forth, looking stupid.

I thought about what to do: Do I take him on and do this full out? No, I decided, I do not want to fight. I just wanted to slap him (hard), and I did it. I was done. I decided it was time to leave.

Shit, the stairway was closed after midnight. I went around the bend where the guys were coming down and ended up facing an elevator. Not good. The guy I called down to slap was on his way, and this other guy was coming after me. What more, they were partners in crime and would unite against me. Standing around waiting for the elevator was not an option. I turned around and went back. "Stay away from me!" I yelled. "I don't want to fight." I automatically switched into English. I also automatically got into my self-defense posture, with both arms up and one leg back.

In a split second, the asshole grabbed both my arms. Shit, I thought, this is not how it happens in my training. Fuck! I panicked. Calm your head, Loolwa, assess the situation.

The reason, I realized, he was able to grab my arms was because I *really* did *not* want to fight. As such, I did not lunge into him when he came at me. In training, I am committed to fighting. If someone makes a motion towards me, I immediately am all over him. In this situation, however, I was trying to *avoid* the situation.

OK, I thought. He's got my arms. Now what.

As soon as I started thinking clearly, I was not afraid anymore. I knew could drop to the ground - thus breaking his grip - and kick the shit out of him. But the other guy might arrive in the middle, I reasoned, and I did not want to get into a multiples fight. I did not feel as at ease and confident in multiples fights as I did in single unarmed assailant fights; *and most importantly, I did not want to get into an all-out fight, because I did not want the police locking me up.*

I decided to continue on the avoidance routine. I easily yanked his grip from my arms - and in doing so realized the extent of my upper body strength. As soon as I got him off me, however, he lunged at me with a kick to my stomach. It stung, but I was not impressed. I have a much stronger kick that can cause significantly more damage. The sting came mostly from the shock of being hit; it never had happened quite like this in my life.

"Get away from me!" I yelled, as I ran towards the stairs leaving the hostel. When I reached the stairway, I stopped and turned around. He was not running after me. "Just leave me alone!" I yelled. At this time, the dork of choice arrived on the scene. "What's going on?" he asked the assailant. I went up to both of them. "What's going on is that I want all of you to leave me alone! You've been harassing me all night. Just get the fuck away from me!" The dork turned to the assailant. "She's crazy," he said.

I realized the situation was out of control, and I began thinking about yelling for security. Suddenly, my eye landed on the words on the assailant's shirt: "Security."

Oh, shit, I thought. Of all the guys I decided to try this hitting thing on, I chose the security guard. *Whoops!* I laughed to myself, taken by the humor and irony of it all.

At this time, I realized that I was in danger. Clearly, there was nobody at the hostel protecting me. I did not feel safe going to the police, because they might throw *me* into the slammer. All my money and possessions were in my room upstairs, and it was too late to just wander around. "Look," I said, "I just want to get past. I don't want to fight. Just let me by." I walked past them, reached the elevator, and pushed the button. The elevator door opened immediately. I stepped in, but the two assailants started coming. There was no way I was going to let them in with me.

They blocked my exit out. I bellowed at the top of my lungs and charged through them, into the clear. "You come over here," I instructed them, "and I'll go in the elevator by myself." "You have nothing to worry about," they said, "Come in. We won't do anything to you." "There's no way in hell I'm getting in there with you," I said. "You come over here, and I'll go up by myself." They kept telling me to come in with them. I decided it was time to leave.

I ran to the fancy hotel next door. "These guys next door were harassing me, and I slapped one of them. He kicked me in the stomach, and now he and his friend won't let me up to the hostel - they're blocking my way to the elevator. Can you have security come over with me, so I can get to my room?" The man was very helpful, immediately beckoning over their own security to escort me back. This security guard came with me as far as the elevator, then said, "I don't feel comfortable coming up, because I do not have authority here, but I'm sure they have a security guard that will take care of you." "Yah," I answered dismally, "I'm sure they do."

I took a deep breath and got into the elevator, anticipating five men waiting to jump me on the other end. I prepared myself for a multiples fight. When the door opened, however, they were clustered around the registration desk. I calmly strode forward, speaking directly and confidently to the security guard. I took a proactive approach, simultaneously stalling for time and asserting that I was not afraid. "I'm going to report you first thing in the morning," I said. I continued walking forward.

"Hey, are you staying here?" they asked. For a fleeting moment, I thought it might be to my advantage to answer yes and play the incensed guest. Perhaps, I thought, they then will be cautious about messing with me and will leave me alone. My gut, however, told me to get out of there as quickly as possible. I continued walking calmly forward, as they fielded questions. "Hey, are you staying here? What room are you in?"

I passed through the door outside, continuing my stride till I turned the corner and out of sight. Then I bolted like hell. Thank G-d/dess my roommate had not locked the door. I swung it open and locked it shut.

Just in time.

I heard them racing down the pathway, right outside my door. "Efo ze?" they yelled. Where is *that*. Not where is she; where is *that*. That dehumanized thing. Thank G-d/dess, thank G-d/dess, I took the right actions. They really were after me. It was unbelievable.

I stayed perfectly still. I dared not give away any signs of life, lest they bust into the room. The security guard, after all, would have the key. My heart pounded. I was scared. I could not leave the room. I could not grab my things and get out of the situation; it was not safe to walk outside. Yet I did not feel safe *in* the room, given my assailant's access to it. I felt literally trapped. There was nothing I could do, nobody I could call, no one to talk to. Except, of course, my tape recorder...

After there was quiet for a few minutes, I started moving about. Each time I heard a sound, though, I turned off whatever light was on and sat perfectly still, listening. In time, I realized other people were awake as well, so it was relatively safe to leave the lights on and make noise. Besides, I locked the doors to the toilet and shower while using them. Even if the assailants poked their heads into various rooms in search of me, I did not think the security guard would risk the consequences of banging on a bathroom door while some unknown person was showering - especially at this hour.

I recorded the events on my tape recorder, while sitting on the toilet. I took a long hot shower, reassuring myself I would make it through this ordeal. I went to bed. I hardly could sleep. I listened hard to the sounds outside.

Finally, I reasoned they were not going to come into every room, searching for me. Even if they managed to enter rooms unnoticed, they would have to check every person in each bed, in the dark. Complaints would abound. I doubted the security guard would risk it. Still, I did not feel safe....

Somehow, I managed to get to sleep, though I can't say I slept well. I woke up frequently, until light came. Even then, it was a fitful sleep, full of nightmares.

Women are unprotected by the very institutions established for the purpose of citizen protection. What more, these institutions *themselves* threaten women's safety:

As I discussed earlier, common and constant forms of male assault against women are socially acceptable and not punishable by law, though they may have the same impact on women as the behavior that currently *is* labeled "violence." Whereas by law a woman physically may defend her space when a man hits her, she is not allowed to do the same when a man aggressively invades her space through other means, such as verbal or visual assault. Women's *non*-physical responses to verbal/visual assault frequently are ineffective or are used to further an assault against us: Men frequently take advantage of and smear our faces in the fact that we do not have institutional power to prevent or counteract such assault.

Given the current legal restrictions, it may be more "appealing" to be assaulted physically; at least then we legally can fight back. To the contrary, no matter how violent and threatening a verbal/visual assault against us may be, *we* will be the ones deemed "assailants" if we strike the first blow.

I find myself more concerned about police response to *my response to assault* than about assault itself. I feel powerful and competent in taking care of myself. I feel the right to my space, and I feel entitled to defending it. With current legal biases, however, defending myself and my space do not usually feel like options. Except in extreme circumstances, my hands feel tied behind my back: Through resisting assault, I may experience more violation by the "justice" system than I may experience by submitting to the assault.

Current laws as such dissuade women from taking care of ourselves in most situations. They not only do not offer us institutional protection in return, but they offer us punishment if we insist on self-protection. As a result, regardless of our level of strength and skill, we still may walk through the world feeling vulnerable and unsafe.

I chose not to fight the security guard for a number of reasons. Foremost on my mind, however, was fear of ending up in jail, where the police might not have any sympathy for me and where I thus might not have any support; technically, after all, I struck the first blow. By effectively taking away my option to fight physically, the system inherently took away my choice of how to defend myself and my space - which in turn stripped me of a certain amount of self-power.

What we have here is a situation where there is no institutional consequence for various levels of male assault of women, yet there is significant consequence for female resistance to such assault. I believe this setup is no accident, for the legal justice system is imbedded - and therefore invested - in patriarchy. The common, daily forms of assault against women are so pervasive that women would threaten the entire foundation of society if we were to resist them. By dissuading women from such resistance, the "justice" system effectively disempowers us from destroying the patriarchal foundation.

Women and men need to work together, both as reformers within the current legal system and as agitators outside the system, to make this society safe for women.

I feel we need to push for new legislation making it legal for women to fight physically against verbal and visual assault. Many questions of course remain, regarding the technical structure for such laws: Should there be specifications for what encompasses verbal/visual assault, for what behavior legally can receive a physical response?

Should a woman be required first to verbally attempt to ward off a verbal or visual assault before launching into physical defense? If so, what should be considered a sufficient attempt: making the statement, "If you do not stop, I will consider this an assault;" saying "leave me alone" - if so, how many times - once, twice...? Should we legislate certain statements as being *offensive* instead of *defensive*, and therefore disqualifying of physical self-defense? If so, what would the statements be - "Fuck off or I'll bash your brains in"?

Should there be limitations on the extent to which a woman physically can respond? For example, she may use her body but not a weapon; she legally cannot knock the man unconscious...? What if the woman hits her assailant just once and intends to stop there, but the man escalates the situation by coming at her full-force or with a weapon?

What should be our criteria for considering and answering all these and the many other questions involved in creating this new legislation?

The levels of male assault against women are staggering. We need to acknowledge the insanity of how frequently men assault women and in how many different ways. We need to make it unacceptable for these assaults to fall through the cracks of our legal justice system. We need to redefine the terms of assault law, taking into consideration the unique character of male assault of women and creating consequence for it.

Women must have the choice of how to protect ourselves from the insanity surrounding us. Currently, we have no acceptable options, except in extreme circumstances.[8] Let us recall there was a time when these extreme circumstances themselves were not considered grounds for "self-defense": For example, it was not acceptable for a woman to fight against rape, since rape was not considered a crime.[9] Assault that today is not considered a crime *also* is a crime; however, women still are the ones paying the price and serving the sentence for it, by being imprisoned in the small scraps of space men "graciously" choose to leave for us.

Verbal/visual assault can come at any time - as I am doing the most mundane things, wearing the most sack-like clothing, and making the least amount of eye contact. I have found, however, that the assault is amped up in direct proportion to my level of freedom and power. The more I express myself, the more shit men throw my way. In this way, verbal/visual assault is consequence to the "audacity" I as a woman have to step out of bounds and take up space fearlessly. As if men could make the "rules." As if women are not "allowed" to be free.

Consequence for female freedom but no consequence for male assault. What is wrong with this picture...

As we work to create new legislation, I believe women need to give ourselves permission to be bold and step beyond the lines of legally acceptable behavior. And I believe everyone supporting female autonomy needs to support the women taking these steps. If a woman is arrested for physically defending herself against verbal/visual assault, for example, activists need to organize protests in support of her self-defense. We need to work on both ends of the stick, resisting current laws while working to change them, creating a ruckus while offering a solution.

There are other ways that systems of "justice" fail to protect women from various forms of assault: For one, we rely heavily on witnesses to confirm that an act of violence actually took place. It is unlikely, however, that there will be witnesses to a rape, given the intimate nature of the crime. We also rely on character witnesses to determine the likelihood that someone would engage in an act of violence. The staggering levels of domestic abuse, however, make it clear that a community do-gooder can be lethal once behind closed doors.

Given the nature of the beast, we need to rethink what measures to use in assessing and punishing male violence against women. We need to acknowledge that an otherwise-pious priest may molest his daughter. We need to acknowledge that a security guard may do a fine job protecting the men in a building yet may assault the women there.

When my hotel escort dumped me at the youth hostel elevator and assured me the security guard would take care of me, I was afraid to identify the security guard as my assailant. Given current measures of assessing violence, "security guard" generally is equated with "protector," conjuring up images of a trustworthy, safe person. As such, the fact that the security guard attacked me may have shed a suspicious light on *me*, rather than on him.

Given the status hype of a security guard, my escort immediately may have assumed that I was at fault. As such, he may have treated me as dangerous, crazy, or both. Given this reality, it felt safer for me to face the security guard alone and take care of myself.

When the individuals society looks up to and turns to for protection are the ones assaulting women; and when, because of their image, those individuals are given more credibility than women, we women are living in a frightening, dangerous situation.

The year I lived in Columbia University housing, a female first year student woke up in the middle of the night to go to the bathroom; and the security guard for the building followed her in and raped her. I am painfully aware this scenario was not unique to Columbia's campus or to the college dorm scene; I know of numerous other parallel scenarios. I myself frequently have felt less safe with security guards than with anyone else in a given building - against whom the security guards supposedly have been there to protect me.

Life's a Beach

When I got up in the morning, I went first thing to the registration desk. My plan was to report the incident, demand my money, and leave the city. The staff, however, was very supportive and encouraged me to stay. The security guard, they informed me, was not an employee; he was hired out from a security agency. They planned to relay my report to the local police and sue the security agency for assault.

I decided to stay at least for the day. After all, I came to Eilat to *relax*.[10] The Red Sea is my favorite place to swim, and I wanted to actually get around to swimming in it.

I went to a pay phone to call home before heading to the beach. As I walked into the courtyard, the security guard's friend appeared out of a nearby elevator. I ran to the front desk and reported him as one of the perpetrators from the night before. As it turned out, he was an employee of the youth hostel, apparently working in maintenance. The assistant manager assured me he would be reprimanded and that I had nothing more to worry about. I went for a swim.

After spending a few hours at the beach, I began ascending the long hill to the central bus station, to pick up a schedule. I figured I would take the last bus out that evening. Starting at a different part of the city than I was used to, I ended up in a residential neighborhood. As I came down one block, two men approached me. "It's hot out today, isn't it?" one of them asked. I did not answer. He repeated himself, this time in English. I still did not answer.

Both men verbally pounced on me simultaneously, calling me this or that because I did not answer them. They in effect staked claims on my space, demanded that I cater to their fancy, and assaulted me for not acquiescing.

I really did not want to get into another row. I continued saying nothing. But as I turned the corner, they jumped in step right behind me. "One! Two! One! Two! One! Two! One! Two..."

...in other words, it was "not an option" for me to choose not to answer. Frequently when men speak with women on the street, it is not about friendliness; rather, it is about dominance. Again, everyone loses out from this violence: As friendly as I and other women may be; as much as we theoretically might be delighted to speak with any given men, we may completely resist being approached by them, out of the probability that we will experience the "same old, same old" twisting of our good will. Friendly, casual connection with men thus becomes nearly impossible for conscious women.

One more thing: These guys did not hesitate to create consequence for my simply keeping *to my own space*. Are women as willing to create consequence for men *invading* our space?

"ENOUGH!" I spun around and yelled at them in Hebrew. *"Enough!"* they mocked me in a high, squeaky voice. I tried to continue walking forward. "You fucking American whore!" they continued in English, following close behind me. "Fuck you, fucking bitch! Fucking American slut!" I was exasperated. All I wanted was to get to the stupid bus station in peace. "Suck my dick, bitch!"

I stopped and faced them. "Back off!" I yelled, getting into fighting stance. *"Back off!"* they responded, again in the high, squeaky voice, putting up their hands as if they were helpless. Now that *really* irritated me. They were mocking my self-defense tone and posture.

I looked at them and weighed my options. From the incident the night before, I learned that I must be willing to go through a full-force fight if I was going to hit someone. Otherwise, I would be putting myself in danger. Which, I asked myself, would be more of an energy drain today: getting into an all-out fight and then having to deal with the police? Or not confronting their harassment? I chose the latter as the best option for the moment. I was tired, and I wanted to rest. Besides, I reasoned, I did not want to be involved in two incidents within 24 hours; the police might not look favorably upon me, as a result...

Considering that assault of women happens every second, it is quite absurd that I should have to worry about being taken seriously for defending myself against more than one assault within 24 hours. I have observed, nonetheless, that it is hard enough for a woman to be taken seriously the *first* time she responds to an assault. If she is to be involved in more than one assault, forget it. Most people invariably will blame her for whatever occurred.

One of the assailants came towards me and placed his hand on my arm. "Don't touch me!' I shouted, as I whipped his arm off. "I'm going to report you to the police," I continued yelling, as I turned and ran down the hill. My assailants had said hello to someone prior to approaching me. I wanted to find him quickly and see if he would tell their names. "The police can suck my dick!" they shouted from up the hill. They still were grabbing their crotches, making gestures towards me. The noise of their assault was incessant. "Suck my dick, bitch! Fucking whore, go to hell!" They continued on and on and on.

I could not find their friend. I asked a man sitting in the bus stop if he knew who these men were. "No," he said. As I walked away, I realized this man had witnessed the whole assault without stepping in. I felt angry.

I stayed where I was, until the assailants were far enough up the hill for me to proceed again towards the bus station. The whole time they climbed the hill, they chortled in delight, laughing at me, reveling in their *power over*, reveling in their ability to assault *without consequence*.

As I recount this scenario, I anticipate readers telling me I should have backed off sooner/gone another direction/returned the way I came...It is daunting to put forth into the universe the concept of a woman taking up and demanding her space, instead of turning around and walking away.

Most people evaluate situations in terms of the way things are now. As such, I believe most would agree that women should *compensate* for the violence against us, by contorting our lives around the little specks of universe we "are given."

I disagree, and it is scary to do so.

I crossed the street and continued up the hill, tears streaming down my cheeks - cheeks that burned with anger. I was stronger than ever before, but I felt so helpless. With hitting as a new option in my repertoire of responses to harassment, I acted powerfully by making a *choice* not to hit. It was the first time where I knew for a fact I could hit if I wanted to, but doing so did not seem worth it.

Still, I felt like shit. They still victimized me.

Yes, I made great choices. Yes, I was powerful in my actions, considering the circumstances. But they still got away with assaulting me. I was in pain and smoldering with anger, and there was nothing I could do to remedy the situation, to bring them to justice. In that sense, I was powerless. They had exercised power over me; and *there was no consequence for their actions*.

At the top of the hill, I sat on a bench and cried, with my head in my hands. After a while, I looked up. One of the assailants started crossing the street, diagonally ahead of me. I could not believe my luck. Was it really him?

I jumped into action. I ran across the street, following him across and down the hill. On the way, I stopped a girl and asked her to call the police for me. I continued following him, jumping into a store when he paused and looked around. I caught the side of his unusually ugly face. It definitely was him. There was no way in hell I was going to let him go.

He turned around and went back up the hill. I followed, stopping at a pay phone to call the police. "These two men were harassing me, and I just saw one of them. He's on [this street], heading in [that direction], and I'm going after him." The operator told me to stay where I was. "I can't," I said. "I'll lose him." I hung up and pursued my assailant. Around the corner, up the hill, across the street, down the next block. I called the police to give an update. "Stay where you are," the operator said again. "I can't, I have to follow him. I'll call you again."

Down the next block, around the corner, up a hill. Whenever I passed a restaurant, I told the man at the counter to call the police and give an update on the whereabouts of my assailant and myself. The restaurant people got very excited by the thrill of the chase and wanted to know details. "I can't talk, I've got to go," I said each time. "Yah," I added in my head, "and you've probably done the same to women many times over, anyhow..." I got quite a rush out of the irony of getting these men to call the police about behavior they probably engage in all the time.

Ten minutes into the chase, the assailant stopped for a drink in a restaurant. I stopped at the restaurant across the street and waited, watching him. I felt as if I were in a movie. At one point, my assailant looked around and saw me. He raised his glass in a toast. Stupid moron was so confident nothing would happen to him, he thought he'd revel a little more in his privilege to harm. "Yah, sweet ass," I thought, "you're in for a toast alright." The joke was on *him*, and *I* reveled in it.

Assailant got up and continued our journey across town. I told kiosk owners and the people in the hardware store to notify the police of our progress. "Where the fuck are they?" I thought to myself. We began entering the seedy part of town. It had been over 20 minutes since the pursuit began. Assailant began entering a skanky-looking bar. Suddenly, a car zoomed up to the curb near me, and four burly men jumped out. "We're the police," they said. "Where is he?" "Over there!" I pointed. "In the turquoise shorts, going into the bar!"

Ya-hoooooooooo! Sweet justice, come my way!

The police jumped back in and zoomed ahead to the bar. I ran diagonally across, my backpack bumping wildly. I arrived just as the police ran up the stairs after Assailant. They took him by the arms, escorted him down the stairs, and handcuffed him, as I watched with delight.

"Now, what was that you said?" I thought to myself, "The police can suck my *what?*" Victory, sweet victory! I laughed hard inside, doing mental cartwheels of celebration.

The police placed Assailant in the car and asked me to stay put; there was not enough room for everyone. As they zoomed off to the station, I looked around at the many faces staring at me from every direction. I felt as though I were in an old Western movie, where all conversation stops after one of the characters enters the bar.

As I became more aware of my surroundings, I realized everyone must be completely stoned. It was surreal. People had thoroughly blank expressions on their faces. I began feeling unsafe. I went to a table with a woman and asked if I could sit with her. My plan was to stay far away from men, so no more incidents would occur between the time the police left and returned. But people kept asking me questions about what happened, and I decided to leave the bar.

I sat on the street corner across from the bar. *Hurry up,* I thought. *Hurry up...* "What did he do?" one man came and asked me. "He must have done something terrible," another added. They began clustering around me. Oh, no, I thought. Just stay away from me until the police come. Just don't bother me for the next five minutes, no more incidents, just five minutes, pleeeeeease...

"I just need peace and quiet right now," I said in a quiet voice. They continued pestering me with questions. "I just need peace and quiet right now. Thank you." They kept talking at me. "Thank you," I repeated. If I kept acting as if they were respecting my boundaries, maybe they actually would. "Thank you...thank you." I put my hand up in a simultaneous thanks/no/goodbye gesture. After saying thanks about five times, the men began leaving. Thank G-d/dess!

The police finally came back to pick me up. I was anxious about their finding out I was the same person who reported the security guard in the morning. For reasons stated previously, I figured that once they knew, their support for me suddenly would vanish.

The police were very friendly to me, and they were completely sympathetic as I described what happened. "Did he touch you?" they asked. I told them he touched my arm, but I whipped it off.

We arrived at the station, and one of the officers escorted me to the sergeant's office. The sergeant was not as friendly as my police chauffeurs, and he insisted that I describe the incident in Hebrew, not English. I wanted to keep him on my side; so after a few attempts to change his mind, I went along with his rules.

The officer who brought me came in and out, and the sergeant and he spoke with each other too quickly for me to know for sure what they were saying. Either they were talking about another man, or this man also had done something - I don't know what - to another woman. I asked for clarification about what was happening. They wouldn't take the time to explain.

They talked about my situation. "Did he touch her?" the sergeant asked the officer. "No." "Then we can't do anything," the sergeant decreed. "But they were grabbing their crotches and screaming, 'Fuck you, bitch!' They may not have hit me, but they were totally assaulting me!" The sergeant and officer talked with each other some more in speedy Hebrew. I did not understand what they said, and they would not tell me. I felt completely shut out, frustrated, and powerless. I bid my case again and again.

Finally, the officer left and did not come back. The sergeant began writing up a report. "So what is happening?" I asked. "We're locking him up," he said. I was not sure I understood the word correctly and asked if that was what he meant. He nodded yes.

I still was not sure whether the sergeant just was not listening to me or they really locked up Assailant. I also had no idea how long Assailant would be in jail even assuming he *was* locked up. But at the very least, I knew I gave Assailant a bad day, and that was enough for me. I went back to the youth hostel feeling satisfied and ready for a swim.

I walked into my room and put down my backpack. Someone knocked at the door. I did not answer, not exactly trusting whom it might be. The visitor knocked again. I still did not answer, but the door opened. The registration clerk for the evening shift walked into my room. "The assistant manager wants you to come with him now to go to the police and file a report about the security guard."

Unbelievable.

"But they said I did not have to do anything, that they were taking care of it all!" I protested. "It will just take a minute, it's just a formality," she said. "They need you to be there in person to file the report." "Can't I do it later?" I practically begged. "I had a hard day, and I just want a swim..." "No, he has to do it now. It will just take a minute."

Exhausted with anxiety, I gathered my belongings and followed the clerk to the front office, shuffling my feet the whole way. *Oh, shit, oh shit, oh, shit,* I thought. I really did not want to go back to the police station. They might throw out my whole case, let Assailant out of the slammer...

Shimon was chipper and friendly, as he closed his office and took me to his car. I felt morose. I tried to convince him to make the report later. At least, I reasoned to myself, I might have a chance of a later shift of police. He could not go later but tried to console me by saying it would just be a minute, a simple procedure, and then it all would be over.

Oh, man, I thought to myself. *Oh, man, oh, man, oh, man...*

Finally I told him. "Look," I said. "There was an incident this morning. These guys were harassing me, and I got one of them put in jail. I'm afraid that if I report two cases in one day, the police will blame it on me; that they won't see my complaints as valid, and they'll throw everything out..." "No, no," Shimon shook his head. "If two things happened in one day, two things happened in one day. That's the way things go sometimes. Besides," he soothed me, "the police know me. I'll tell them what happened. You'll be with me, and everything will be OK."

I felt comforted by Shimon's words. I was quite surprised by his attitude. I thought for sure he would not back me anymore, after hearing about the second incident. With his unwavering support, I felt more confident in the legitimacy of my complaints; and I began to believe it was possible that the police would not respond the way I anticipated.

Another man was in the car with us, and he questioned the fact that these two incidents happened. "Look," Shimon responded to him, "Some guys are like that. This stuff happens." The man took in the statement like new information, without challenging it.

I barely was breathing when we reached the police station. The officers who had brought me to the station were in a jeep at the entrance, on their way out. They looked at me with surprise and questioned Shimon. He went over to talk with them, then came back to the car, assuring me everything would be OK. I still was anxious.

We waited in the hallway in front of the sergeant's office, and I chatted it up with two British tourists whose wallets were stolen on their last day in the country. After twenty minutes, the sergeant called them into the office. Shimon and I continued waiting. A line formed in the waiting "room" chairs. One by one, people who had arrived after me were called in before me. In time, it became clear I was being ignored.

Shimon left and returned several times, as a combined result of talking with the officers and running back to the hostel for brief errands. When I asked various people what was going on, I was ignored or given confusing answers I did not understand. But I felt in no position to push anyone for action. I was emotionally fatigued; and moreover, I was afraid of being seen as a troublemaker and thus "the cause of" the assaults against me.

So I just waited...And waited.

In time, the sergeant came out and told one of the officers to "explain to [me] what's going on." The appointed man took me outside, leaned against the railing, and looked out over the parking lot. "The security guard filed charges against you." *Oh, shit,* I thought. I feared being locked up or detained in the country. "*What?!*" I said in an exasperated tone. "*He* filed charges against *me?!*" In truth, I cannot say I was surprised, but I decided it was best to play it that way.

The officer - one I had not yet met - seemed completely disinterested in what I had to say. What more, he seemed quite pleased with his news. Given his tone and mannerism, I easily could imagine him saying, "Listen, little girl, we're gonna get you..." He spoke to me in an intimidating way, implying that if I pressed charges, I would be the one locked up. "That's just the situation," he said dismissively. "I'm just telling you."

He seemed amused by my distress, as he sauntered back into the station.

I wanted to cry. I was exhausted. I just wanted to get the hell out of Eilat. I just wanted to be somewhere safe.

I dragged myself back into the waiting room, where Shimon was chain smoking like a madman. At least, I thought, I want to be outside, enjoying the sun and air. I asked if he would mind if I waited outside. He did not and promised to tell me when it was my turn.

Hours passed. I went in and out, in and out of the station. Shimon smoked and smoked. I asked the sergeant when he would see me and why so many people were put ahead of me. He said he was busy and that I could wait indefinitely now or come back later in the night. I did not want to have this issue hanging over my head; I did not want to deal with the situation without Shimon there; and I did not even know if the sergeant would see me later if I did return, as it was clear he was trying to get rid of me. I asked various staff for an explanation of what was happening. Everyone gave me the brush-off.

I knew the hour was coming when Shimon would have to go back to the hostel. I sat on a rock outside and looked at the Red Sea, spread out invitingly just a mile in front of me. All I wanted to do was swim. I just wanted to rest...The sun was setting, and I breathed in the rainbow of colors. *I can center myself anywhere*, I thought. *I can enjoy life anywhere, anytime. There is no excuse for misery as a result of someone else's bullshit.* I began a mild form of dance/prayer, rejoicing in the glory around me. I was cautious, however, about the extent of my visible joy. I did not want any more incidents, and I did not want the officers seeing me and declaring me as "crazy."

Where there is life, there frequently is fear. It is a sad commentary on our society that one might be called "crazy" for rejoicing in the beauty around; for standing up for herself against assault; for generally demanding to be robust in her senses and her space.

Where there is life, there frequently is punishment. It is frightening that individuals randomly bestowed with the title of "authority" - in this case, the police - can feel threatened personally by someone's freedom and can have the power to restrain that person, thus removing her from the fountain of life and damaging her soul...

In time, I sat back down on the rock and considered my options. I could, I reasoned, stay at the station. I could make sure charges were filed against the security guard, and I could leave Eilat feeling finished. At the same time, I might end up being stuck at the station for the rest of the evening. And there was no guarantee the sergeant actually ever would see me. What more, the sergeant was not my ally. Even if he did see me, the situation might get worse, and Shimon would not be there to support me.

I did not want to get caught in the *thing* of reporting the security guard, to the extent that it was beyond my interest and trapping me in someone else's agenda. "What do *I* want, right now?" I asked myself. I was mentally and emotionally spent. I just wanted to go to the beach, relax, and enjoy what was left of the day.

I realized that I already had accomplished everything *I* wanted: I slapped the security guard - one of the highlights of my life - and I put the afternoon asshole in jail - yet another highlight. I was satisfied. I had done enough. Yes, it would be nice to create legal and professional consequence for the security guard, but I did not need it to happen. *I already had fought and won the battles that concerned me.*

To stay at the station and be unhappy; to spend hours of my vacation engaged in this miserable battle, I reasoned, would be contrary to taking care of myself. Besides, I could continue the fight after resting, from a safe space. I could get my friend's lawyer father to call and follow up on the situation. For the moment, it was time to swim.

I went in the station and asked Shimon if I could have a lawyer call and follow up on the incident, so I would not have to stay. He said yes, and I told him I preferred that action. We left the station.

I spent the night recuperating in the moonlit waters of the Red Sea, and I returned to the youth hostel, calm and refreshed.

I went upstairs to the mini-store/cafe on the rooftop. The maintenance guy - one of my assailants from the night before - was sitting on a countertop stool. I looked at him steadily, before turning my attention to the ice cream bin on the side closest to me. As I considered the options, the guy behind the counter excitedly approached me. "Aren't you the one who was dancing last night?" I looked up and recognized him as the third of my five harassers. Good god, were all my assailants employees? "No," I replied evenly. I rummaged through the ice cream some more, but I had lost my appetite. I left.

I was choked with anger and hurt. It was such a game to him, and it was so traumatic to me. Like boys playing with a little mouse, thinking it was so cute to swing her by the tail as she screamed in terror. I decided to go back up and get his name, and I did so. After wandering around a little longer, I decided it was time to get to sleep. I was taking the first bus out the next day and had to wake up at 5 am.

In the morning, I went to the registration desk to check out. Assailant #4 turned out to be the late night/early morning clerk. It was out of control already. I knew, however, he would not bother me, considering I was pressing charges. I asked for my information card, making some excuse for why I needed it. When he gave it to me, I scratched out all the address/telephone information on it. He got very upset, saying he would get in trouble without that information. I compromised by putting a fake number in its place.

I left the youth hostel and got the fuck out of Eilat.

When people perceive us in a certain way, it often is hard to maintain clarity about who we are. While in Eilat, I had difficulty *not* perceiving myself as an assailant, given my (proven) expectation that others would see me that way. As someone pushing the envelopes of female response to male violence, I not only had to fight the battles against the violence itself; but I had to fight the attitudes towards me, in response to my behavior. It is scary and difficult to put forth ideas and behavior not yet understood or accepted by society. It was

hard for me to do while in Eilat; and for reasons mentioned
before, it is hard for me to do now.

Options and Opportunities

Two years earlier, as I traveled through Israel, I met and fell in love with a free-spirited art student, Gil Tselner. We had a "soul mate" kind of connection, and the circumstances around our meeting were too many and too coincidental to appear less than fated by the universe. I felt this person could be my life partner; and two months after returning to the States, I risked everything - including every cent I had - to fly halfway across the world to be with him again.

He raped me.

I didn't call it rape at the time; I was confused. He began penetrating; I said no; and he stopped. Literally one minute later, he asked, "Do you want me?" "No," I said. *What do you mean, "Do I want you?"* I thought. *I just SAID no.* A few minutes later, he began penetrating again; I said no; and he stopped. *Maybe he doesn't feel it going in,* I thought.

We were being pretty sexually active without having intercourse. I allowed for the possibility that he just did not notice quite where his penis was. A few times, after all, he did readjust himself, without my saying anything. But the times he did not reposition himself, it felt certain he would have kept going, despite the fact I clearly stated I did not want intercourse.

I felt violated by the experience, but I did not feel the power to confront it until the day I left. Still, I did not call it rape; though I did call it "violence." A few weeks after returning to the States, I thought, "Rape is defined as penetration without consent. What is the difference? Technically, it was rape."

In consensual sex, I reasoned, I am not the sole individual looking out for my boundaries. Once I state them, my partner is as responsible for observing them as I am. It is war, not sex, if I must be *on guard* all the time; if I must state and restate my boundaries, as my "partner" attempts to slip by them, change them, or wear them down.

Most of my sexual experiences with men have involved some level of violence - namely, the men have initiated sexual acts through using my body in some way, without my consent. And when I have said no, many have stopped momentarily, only to engage in the same behavior minutes later.

Where would I tolerate degrees of violence, and where would I draw the line? And how would I respond to the violence that happened? I thought about and partially discussed these questions as I was with Gil.

It is confusing how men[11] can transition from being lovers to violators, in one single moment, with one single movement. Where do we as women continue treating our "partners" as trusted people, saying, "he needs to learn/he just doesn't get it/this thing is not such a big deal"? Where do we give our lovers slack and discuss our feelings with them? How many chances do we give them? Where do we draw the line and say no, this behavior is unacceptable? Where do we physically fight? And what criteria do we use in assessing our choices for responses?

Specifically, should I have given Gil slack for the possibility that he was not aware of (or paying attention to) where his penis was? Or was it unacceptable enough that he was not being more aware? Should I have stopped being intimate with him as soon as he began penetrating?[12] If I should have stopped, should I have discussed the situation with him; left his apartment; stopped speaking with him; reported him to the police? Should I have hit him, the moment he began penetrating? Or would hitting him only have been an acceptable option if he had continued penetrating *as* I said, "Stop"? Acceptable according to what or whom?

When we speak about rape, we often gloss over the subtleties and complexities of it. In so-called "date rape," there is a gray area where energy begins shifting from intimacy to violence. At that shifting point, I feel women have the right to hit if we so desire. Regardless of whether or not we choose to do so, the law needs to back us up, so that we have the *option*.

After all, who currently pays the price for which behavior? Based on my knowledge of how rape cases are handled, I cannot imagine the police would have paid any attention to what Gil did. I can, however, imagine them giving me significant trouble for hitting him. It seems to me that legal justice systems take rape seriously only as defined by extreme and narrow parameters. I believe my hitting Gil would have been considered "self-defense" only if he had tried pinning me to the bed and forcing his penis *all* the way in, *as* I screamed loudly in protest.[13] So where is the consequence for sexual behavior that is still violent but not quite that extreme?

In legal self-defense, a certain amount of violation must occur before it is considered acceptable to meet the violation with physical force. As I mentioned earlier, the most common and persistent forms of violence towards women fall just short of that place - and deliberately so. Given this reality, women are in a legal bind that paralyzes us and prevents us from fighting against violent behavior. In other words, by not seriously or adequately addressing the nature of male violence against women, the law effectively protects and endorses it.

We need to change the law.

Most people seem to think only in terms of the way things are today: What are our options *under the framework of the current system?* How can we as individuals deal with difficult situations in ways that use the least amount of energy and cause us the least amount of harm? It is important to take today's reality into consideration, so as to evaluate wisely our choices of how to behave. It is limited and dangerous, however, to use the current system as our *point of reference for defining* acceptable and unacceptable behavior.

As a result of limited thinking, there is confusion between what are practical strategies and personal preferences for dealing with sexual violence as it exists today and what are women's *rights* of how to be able to behave and what to be able to expect from others. Based on this confusion, society ends up holding women accountable for the violence perpetrated against us.

For example, I am a very flirtatious and sexual person by nature; and I would love to share sexual energy with many different men. Given, however, the way violence is weaved into heterosexual sexuality, I have learned not to get involved with a man unless I know him very well. I believe my choice is wise, considering the reality of how things are today. But I should not *have* to make this choice. I *should* have the room to be wildly flirtatious and overtly sexual and to get physically involved with a man from the moment I feel the desire to do so. *Violence never should enter the picture, period.*

Rather than looking at what I or other women should or should not do, *as based on the sexual violence that already exists,* society needs to consider how to support women in making the choices we want and deserve to be able to make. Violent men need to be the ones holding the burden of their actions, not innocent women.[14] Women must no longer be forced into a position where, given the circumstances of current reality, our wisest choice constantly is to avoid, withdraw, leave, give it up, hand it over...

We need to maximize the consequence for perpetrators of sexual violence and minimize the consequence for women fighting it. If we as women know that we will be *backed up,* not punished, for taking up our space, I guarantee we will take it up and thus nip violence in the bud.

Prior to going to Israel on this trip, I had told two friends I anticipated running into Gil. The whole country was small enough for it to happen. What more, Gil lived in downtown Jerusalem, which was only a few blocks long. I definitely did not want to walk around avoiding him, hiding.

So I discussed possibilities of how to approach Gil and the issue of his raping me. I wanted to be strong enough, committed enough to *myself,* that I would be willing to beat him up if I saw him. What's more, I had the key to his apartment; and I considered doing him or his apartment premeditated damage.

I was terrified to think about these possibilities, because I knew how most people would assess my behavior if I went through with it: They would call me violent, crazy, etc, etc, etc. *Why?*

Whether legally sanctioned or not, it seems to be socially acceptable and understandable that if a man rapes a woman, her male lover, friend, or family member will seek retribution on her behalf. Why does it not seem as (or more!) acceptable and understandable for a woman to seek retribution on her own behalf - especially when the legal justice system will not stand against the violence that happened to her?

Our society encourages men to protect their bodies and space; to address grievances committed against them; and to punish the perpetrators of such grievances. To the contrary, our society encourages women to tolerate endless invasion of our bodies and space and to forgive the perpetrators of these invasions. On this model, a man can protect "his woman" but a woman cannot protect herself - as in, *what* self do we by social definition *have* to protect?

Even where it is socially or legally acceptable for a woman to engage in physical combat *while* she is being attacked, it is not condoned once a man finishes assaulting her. But what if a woman does not have the emotional or physical strength to fight her assailant as he attacks her? What if she does not have the understanding at the time that what is happening to her is violence? What if she realizes the nature of the situation and musters up the physical/emotional strength only *after* the assault happens? Why should the assailant be the one determining the timetable and parameters of the fight?

What if the legal justice system provides no recourse for the woman after the assault, given current definitions of what is punishable by law? Should the perpetrator walk away with no accountability or consequence for his actions? What if going through the system would further victimize the woman? Should she endure more trauma trying to work through an unsympathetic system, where statistical chances are the perpetrator will go unpunished anyhow? Where is the justice here?

I wanted to work myself to the point that I would be *willing* to do something physical, something painful, something with impact in response to Gil. I wanted to take my female body and self seriously enough that I would take his behavior seriously enough to make *him* be the one bearing the burden of his actions, on *my* timetable, regardless of social or legal rules and restrictions. "Some things don't come full circle," a woman's punk rock group sings in a song about violence against women.[15] Why should we always be the ones always left holding the bag?

I believe that in certain contexts, there *is* healing strength in fighting. For men, who traditionally will fly off the handle and pummel someone's brains out at the drop of a hat, I believe learning *not* to fight is where healing strength lies. For women, who constantly are "peacemakers" at our own expense, I believe *fighting* is where healing strength lies.

To see all fighting as violent and counter-productive, I believe, is to see it in a male context only. To live in true peace, I believe men need to stop over-fighting, and women need to stop under-fighting. We have to meet in the middle, where there is balance. Where there is balance, I believe, there is true peace.

Before I left the States, one of my friends suggested that I not go after Gil. She thought I should utilize the shift in my consciousness for a future commitment to hitting men in the moment of assault. Though she agreed with the unfairness of the situation with Gil, she felt my doing damage to his apartment or beating him up in the street would be too risky for me. Not only would I be doing something unsanctioned by society, but I would be doing it in another country, where I would not have my support system behind me.

As I continued reflecting on my options, I saw the wisdom in my friend's advice; and I decided not to go to Israel with the *intention* of doing something Gil. I knew that a plan to hurt him would consume me during my entire trip, and I did not want to give him that much energy. I also knew my friend was right about the odds being stacked against me; and I reasoned that Gil would inherently take even more from my life if I ended up in jail because of him. The risk of what I had to lose seemed greater in this situation than what I had to gain. I decided to let go of the issue for the time being and to let myself live in the moment, see what happened once I got to Israel.

Having escaped from Eilat, I went to Jerusalem for the holy day of Shbuoth.[16] After settling in a youth hostel, I hurried to the central shouk,[17] to buy fruits and vegetables before everything closed. As I wound around a corner in the market, I *literally* bumped into Gil. He did not see me, and the market was packed. The situation seemed perfect: I could knee him in the groin, stomp on his feet, sock him in the face...and get away, without his knowing what or who hit him.

After considering the possibility, I chose not to hit Gil. First, I wanted him to know *I* was the one hitting him. I did not want to hit and run, making him think he got randomly mugged in the shouk. Second, I wanted Gil to know *why* I was hitting him. I wanted him to comprehend that my hitting him was the consequence of his actions. I wanted him to understand the violence of his actions. [18]

Third, I did not want consequence for *my* actions. I did not want to risk the unknown. I needed peace and quiet, and I did not want to deal with an uproar, possibly arrest. Fourth, I knew I *could* hit Gil if I wanted. It had become an actual option, not a fantasy. I had hit other men by that point; I already had succeeded in pushing the envelope. And I just did not feel like putting out the energy at that moment.

It is incredible that I ran into Gil (literally) only after I had the experiences of hitting the other men. I had been in downtown Jerusalem a number of times before; but I never saw him until that time.

Holy Hell

The next day, I left the youth hostel and went into the Old City for religious programs. Crossing a street on my way back, two or three men blocked my way. I moved to the right, and they moved there. I moved to the left, and they moved in that direction. "STOP!" I yelled. They laughed at succeeding to upset me, as I walked in an extra-wide arc around them.

I went out of *my* way, *around* these men. Again, they found it funny when I yelled at them; it all was part of the power trip. My words were no consequence to their behavior. How much better just to hit men like this, make *them* pay the price for their behavior! If only there were not so many factors currently involved, making it a huge risk for women to do...

The next afternoon, I walked from the youth hostel to the Old City, for another religious program. *Beep, beep!* I looked at the autos stopped at the red light. One was a police on a motorcycle. "Hello, sweetie!" our helmeted hero shouted. The situation was so ridiculous, it was far beyond upsetting; and I thought I would explode in laughter. The light turned green, and Dick Squad pulled up next to me. "Hello, cutie, how are you?" No answer. "Where are you going?" Still no answer. He followed me. "Do you want a ride?" I kept walking. Eventually, he went away. *Oh, my god,* I thought, *this world is crazy. There is nobody protecting the women. Nobody.*

Evening fell, and I was in the popular courtyard square of the Jewish Quarter. Standing on the edge of a lawn, I began moving my arms skyward and swinging my body slightly, in prayer communication with the Creator.

"Is that a dance?"

The soldier was like a fly zooming in on a spot of honey. I did not answer. He asked again.

"Could it be," I responded mockingly, *"that this is a...* DANCE??????" I made dramatic gestures with my body. *"Tell me!"* I ran up close to him, *"is that a DANCE you are*

doing? Is it POSSIBLE..." I burst open my eyes in mock excitement, as I started running around. *"that this is...a* **DANCE???????"**

Now, THIS was fun.

"Excuse me!" I pursued without mercy. *"What are you DOING? Could it be...that you are* **DANCING??????"** I laughed hard, my head thrown back. I expanded so fully in my grace and my fun that my joy became a counter-assault. "You're crazy," the soldier mumbled, shuffling away. *"But wait!"* I swung around to face him. *"What IS that? Is it...a* **DANCE????"** I turned back around, leaping in the air. *"Tell me, what are you DOING??????...Are you...DANCING??????"* I laughed and laughed, chortling in delight, yulyulating in connection with the G-ddess, the night, the stars, the rich dark sky...

"Can I ask you a question?" An American teen approached me. "No." I continued dancing. The teen continued with his question. I whipped around at him. *"Do you understand English?"* I yelled. "I said *NO*. That means I do NOT want you to ask me a question. Now get away from me." He retreated immediately, as I continued in my connection with the Creator...

Just Call Me "Prof"

I entered a bar in Tiberias, exhausted from weeks of battle. The music playing was irresistible, and I wanted to dance. Badly. But I just couldn't face the prospect of more men harassing me.

Out of nowhere, a woman dressed head-to-toe in purple alighted on the dance platform, placed a menorah (Jewish candelabra) squarely on the top of her head, and began dancing around in a sacred, sensual way.

WOW!

I watched in amazement and inspiration, as the guy behind the counter told me the woman was the local crazy person "but very intelligent, really smart..." *Yah, you repressed moron,* I thought, *she's no crazy person; she's free. She's freer than you, and she's even freer than me...*

As she finished her dance and stepped down from the stage, I ran up to her. "I have GOT to meet someone like you," I said. We began talking. "My mother is an Ethiopian Jew," she said, "and my father is African-American. I grew up in Hawaii..." "Wait!" I squealed, "You're Frani's friend!" Frani Ruch is a soulmate and another wild woman. Like me, she dances on the wind and in the street, at all hours, singing at the top of her lungs, celebrating life. She and this woman, Ovadia, had met and hung out in Israel, two years earlier. Frani had told me stories about her. It was incredible.

We took a table and ordered greasy fries. "Tell me," I said, "how do you continue going? I mean, whenever I am *alive,* guys just zoom in and harass me. I can't move without them saying something." Ovadia looked at me steadfastly. "Loolwa," she said, "you are fire. People are attracted to fire. You can't help it. Wherever you go, whatever you do, you *will* be the center of attention. That's just the way it is.

"Now what I do," she continued, "is I see myself as a professor. I am the Professor of the 'University of Tiberias,' and all the people in this city are my students. You are also a professor. Wherever you go, see people as your students, and see yourself as teaching them. Because you *are* teaching people how to be alive.

"For example, when I walk down the street, guys say, 'Hey Baby.' I turn to them and correct them, telling them it's, 'Hey *Professor.'* I am training them. Most of the guys say, 'Hey Professor,' when they see me now. At first, people saw me as crazy, but now they are getting used to me; and they are supporting me."

I asked her about fighting, about hitting men. She told me of a time that a group of Arab men came and harassed her and a friend, when the two women were sitting in the street, singing songs and prayers. "Their energy was really intense," she said, "and they were challenging our space as Jews, saying we did not have the right to be there. One of the men came towards me. I jumped on a ledge and struck him with a menorah, causing him to gash and bleed. I said, 'This is the land of Athonai [Jewish G-d], not Allah [Muslim G-d]! You have your land, and we have ours. This is the land of Athonai. Go away!' I walked back and forth on that ledge, yelling at him. I was centered. I was protecting my space. I was ready to fight. A crowd gathered, and they supported me. The men went away...'"

Ovadia continued to tell me how a number of men approach and begin talking at her when she sings. "I say, 'Shhh. Listen...'" She placed her finger demonstrably to her lips. "'This is the time to *listen,* not to talk. You are welcome to stay here. But you must just sit and *listen...*' I keep repeating it until they stop talking. Then they stay quietly and listen to me sing...'"

Ovadia and I eventually went dancing together, and I stayed until 2:00 AM. We then said goodbye, and I began walking back to my youth hostel, energized by this injection from another wild woman - one who's over 50 years old and still going, at that! As I passed an open store, I just knew the guy in the doorway was going to start with me. "Hello..." he began.

"Laaaaaaaaaaaaaaaaaaaaaaaaaa!!!!!!!" I sang in a huge, jubilant voice. I drowned out him, his voice, and his energy. I laughed wildly, elated by my new, fun, positive formula for fighting harassment. "She's crazy," he said, withdrawing back into the store.

A group of guys was down the path in front of me. I sensed they would try to possess my singing. And they did try; but I was a step ahead. I turned a corner and went down a different street, instead of passing them. And I *yelled*. Really loud. They stopped bothering me.

Although singing and randomly yelling was more fun than fighting with guys who harassed me, it still took energy - energy I did not feel like expending. "I don't want to have to spend my time doing this when I don't feel like it," I thought. Sigh. Is there no end to the insanity?

Living on the Edge

      I was in the mountains of Sfat, a town with a dominating ultra-Orthodox population. According to the rules of this community, women must be covered from head to toe, wearing only dresses or shirt/skirt combinations; they may not sing unless in unison with other women; and they may not dance except in women's circles. As I sat at the edge of a mountain in my shorts and t-shirt, singing and moving around in a prayer dance by myself, two non-religious men came and started talking at me. "Hello, what are you doing..." I did not respond for a while, but they were (surprise, surprise) persistent.

      "You are welcome to join me," I said, "but I do not want to talk right now. You are welcome to sit and listen." The younger of the two men sat right next to me. "You are welcome to join me, but I want my space. Please sit over there." I motioned farther away from me. The guy moved an inch. "No," I said. "Over there." I pointed. He scooted over significantly, giving me all the space I desired. He did not even put up a fuss. I was surprised.

      I continued singing. The two men just sat and quietly listened to me for about 10 minutes. "You have a beautiful voice," they said before they got up and left.

      I feel this situation was yet another example of where men want to reach out to women but are not willing to put themselves in vulnerable positions; so they reach out in aggressive ways. Through my experimental approach towards these men, it seems I was able to touch their humanness - their desire to connect - and receive the positive they offered, while setting strong boundaries and keeping away the negative.

      It was vulnerable for these men to just sit and listen to me sing, to say I had a beautiful voice. And it was in that very place of their vulnerability that I actually appreciated their company and felt the desire to connect with them. Had they approached me that way from the beginning, I probably would have wanted to talk with them and get to know them. But their initial aggressive approach put me on the defensive and made me want distance. Again, the irony is that men actually may push more women away by refusing to approach us with the vulnerability of respect.

Though these men responded positively to my new approach, I do not know that such an approach necessarily would work on every man or in every situation. And though this approach does seem to have important benefits, its drawback is putting the woman in the position of teacher - i.e., "professor." What if a woman does not want to teach a man about courteous behavior? And what if she does not want male company *at all, i*n any given situations?

Shortly after these men left, several guys passed by in a car, honking and whistling at me. Set against the backdrop of the restrictive ultra-orthodox community of Sfat, I realized the qualitatively different feel between street harassment at the hands of secular men and religious men: Religious men tried to prevent me from taking up my space, whereas secular men got in my space.[19] Religious men tried to silence me, an act requiring my complicity, whereas secular men objectified me, an action out of my control.

By trying to impose their rules on my body; by trying to restrict my movement and define it as a violation of their space, religious men gave *me* all the power. Through dancing, singing, and other forms of expression, I would be violating *their* boundaries, as opposed to them violating mine.

Of course, the religious men's restrictions are harmless only as long as the government does not back them. In holy sites such as the Kotel[20], the government does enforce ultra-orthodox dress and behavior codes for women. At this site, women have been beaten by religious men and arrested by the government, simply for praying out loud.

Perhaps we can take this difference in potency as an example of the extent to which government backing can make or break women's safety in the world. If the government did not currently accept and inherently endorse the forms of sexual assault it does, the world would be a much better place for women.

A crowd of children formed at the foot of a building 50 feet to my right. They stood facing me, listening to me sing. I was shocked they just listened, without trying to silence me. Numerous times at the Kotel, when I danced and sang at the top of my lungs (and when I wore my shorts and sleeveless shirt), children as well as adults had come over to silence me...

In time, the crowd thinned, but two girls remained. "These are going to be the rebels of the community," I smiled to myself. I felt they wanted to approach me. As they began walking away, I wished them Shabbat Shalom[21], to encourage them to come over. "Shabbat Shalom," they responded, seemingly caught off guard. Perhaps they did not expect such religious awareness coming from someone breaking all the rules...

The girls disappeared for a few minutes. Out of nowhere, they were next to me, standing shyly. We began talking, and I invited them to sing and dance with me. They looked like they really wanted to join but said they did not want to. I knew why but asked anyhow, and we got into a discussion about Orthodox restrictions on females.

"We are not allowed to dance," one of the girls said. "What is dancing?" I challenged her. "You're allowed to walk, right?" "Yes," she said. I jumped up and started walking, with my hands swinging at my sides. "Well, what's the difference between this..." I started moving my hands in circles and waves. "...and this?" I began moving my legs in deeper, slower gestures. "At what point..." I began moving my arms in the same motion as my hands. "...does my walk become a dance?" I began moving my torso from side to side and circularly. "And who is going to decide that?" I stopped, looked at her, and sat back down. "These are restrictions men are placing on our bodies, and they don't make any sense."

I can reach down and touch my toes. Period. No expression, no thought, no feeling. Or I can reach my arms up towards the sky, breathe in the air with a wild look in my eyes, smile, twirl my wrists, and sing, as I stretch over and make contact with my feet.

I can jog - put on my walkman, zone out from the world, and run, run, run, stone-faced and staring straight ahead. Or I can skip, smell the flowers, stop to hug some trees, say hello to people I pass, and sing at the top of my lungs.

I find that most of us walk around like robots, so that people will have nothing to take from us: As a result of the primary deaths most of us experienced in early childhood - "stop yelling/stop running/stop acting stupid/stop asking questions..." we learned to squish the life out of ourselves before anyone else could do it to us. If we are lifeless, we think, nobody will be able to kill us again.

As a result, I find that the world often responds hostilely to people who are full of joy or who express intense emotion. Rather than face the pain of what we lost and the challenge of getting it back; rather than join in with and learn from those who still are full of zeal, most of us seem to prefer to snatch from others the life that was snatched from us.

This reality gets intensified in a male-female dynamic: Not only is there a general social drive to keep raw spirit at bay; but it is coupled with an urgent desire to keep women under male control, to stifle the female life force. In my personal experience, men most intensely begin assaulting me at the place where Life bubbles in me, on the line of distinction between *moving* and *living*. They respond either in an attempt to stomp out my vibrancy and freedom or in an attempt to *possess* both qualities and control my spirit. They do not simply honor my space and my power.

What's more, I find that society endorses this behavior towards "wild women," for the reasons mentioned above: Just about everyone has some vested interest in keeping others as stifled as themselves. As such, there is true danger for a woman to be ALIVE in the world: She walks in a hostile reality, where sexist violence against her may be justified by both men and women as being rightful punishment for her being "out of line." The only way to heal this social sickness is through deep personal, political, social, and spiritual revolution.

Go With the Flow

I was on the beach in Tel Aviv, splashing through the waves. Up ahead on the surf, I noticed a girl about seven years old, dancing sensually with her hips circling about and her arms outstretched and twirling in the air. I recognized the dance, having done it myself many times before. She was connecting with nature - the wind, the ocean, the sand, the sky. She was participating in the flow, the high, the energy of the glorious Life force all around her. She was at one with her body, her soul, and the Creator.

And if she was ten years older, you can bet men would be swarming around her, invading her space, claiming her sensual freedom for themselves, poisoning her dance. Whistling, clapping, hooting, talking at her incessantly, asking her over and over again, "What are you doing?"

I stopped and watched this wonderful spirit from a distance, awed and inspired. I felt fear on her behalf: The invasion and gradual erosion of her soul and physical/psychic space inevitably would start as soon as she hit puberty. I prayed to G-ddess to keep her strong enough to defend herself against the assault; to watch over her; to protect her; and never to let her lose her grace, her power of alignment with her Creator and herself.

True female sexuality, our core sexuality - power, confidence, grace, exuberance, self-possession, self-love, celebration, intuitive knowing, connection with the Life force - is beaten out of us from a very young age. It is replaced with a male-constructed, fetishized, one-dimensional, other-oriented parody of the real thing.

This girl's sensuality and sexuality was *for* nobody else. It simply *was*. It simply was *her*, expressing, emoting, being. I believe female sexuality is this way in its natural state - so that even if a woman directs her energy towards someone, she is the actor, the director, the doer. It is for *her*. Once a girl hits puberty, however, men define and claim anything sensual and sexual about her. In this way, they manipulate the root of female power into a tool for power *over* women.

A few years ago, I realized on a deep level that men do not have a vaginal opening. Obviously, I was aware of this phenomenon since I was about two years old - when after going to the bathroom with a boy, I ran out screaming, "Mommy, Jonathan has a tail!" But only a few years ago, I realized the implications.

My vagina not only is my root energy source, but it is my opening to the world. *I am open*. Air flows *through* me. I can feel wind, water, earth, and heat *through* my body. *I am open*. And no man has this opening. It was mind-blowing to realize. And then it all made sense:

This opening is the root of my power. The Life force begins in this place in me. It is my connection to the universe. And what is rape? Why is it such a common form of subordinating women? It is the stuffing up, the plugging, of this opening. It is the interception, the cutting off of this powerful, primary connection to the universe. It is an act of energetic suffocation, spiritual murder.

I find it no accident that many women contract our vaginal area - squeeze it shut - when men verbally / visually assault us. Such assault has the same energetic dynamic, the same *intention*, as rape. It simply comes packaged in a different physical manifestation. When this assault happens, we need to strengthen the flow from our power source outward, rather than contract inward. To contract inward is to allow the suffocation to happen, to physically accept the violent energy, to take it *into* our system - our energy, our body, and thus our emotion and psyche.

What does it mean to strengthen the flow from our power source outward? It essentially means to "go with the flow," which may mean engaging in physical combat with whoever is attacking. It means never leaving our place of power. It means total commitment to ourselves. It means living in our root, 24/7. [22] It means being ALIVE, instead of just getting by. Is that not dangerous to do? Yes. But did we really come here just to get by, on someone else's terms? We must live in the place of danger, if we are to transform it; if we are to learn the specific nature of the threats against us, so that we strategically can eliminate those threats.

Does it mean we physically will fight all the time? Not necessarily. Given that we are limited beings, that assault happens constantly, and that there are real consequences to our actions, we as individuals will need to respond differently in different situations. By becoming *willing* to fight, however, to defend our space and our souls, we can become aware of how much they are under attack every single day. We can become aware of just how much violence we have been taking in. We can become aware of how many times our fighting would be justified and spiritually transformative. And we can become aware of the forces dissuading us from responding instinctually. By operating from our root, with our power radiating outward, our eyes and our minds can open; and we can make *conscious choices*. Conscious choice, I believe, is where freedom, power, and the promise of transformation lie.

This girl's sensuality and sexuality must be protected. There must be the room for her to *expand*, not contract, as she grows. We must insist on this space for each of ourselves, as well. We each must reclaim that dance, demand the room to dance it, and see what happens when we do.

More Feminist Falafel

I revisited the falafel stand in Jerusalem and ordered my regular shwarma. I wondered if the man behind the counter would recognize me. "You're not agitated today?" he said smiling, as he sliced meat from the spit. "No," I responded, "there are no guys in the store to bug me today." "That's true," he laughed, nodding sagaciously. An older man sitting at one of the tables - presumably a friend of the owner's - wanted to know what we were talking about. I grew tense with apprehension. "There were two guys in here the other day," the man behind the counter responded, "and they were treating her very unacceptably." He shook his head in disgust, reflecting on the incident. *"Very* unacceptably." The man at the table took in the information and went back to his paper.

I was stunned.

And elated. The owner was backing me! He felt the wrong behavior was on the part of the guys who harassed me, not me. I felt so validated. I am used to people responding on a model of "woman-should-do-no-harm," seeing women's response to violence as being the violence itself. I felt a bond with the owner, and it was especially comforting that he was an older Mizrahi man.[23]

What Are You Doing?

A few days before leaving Israel, I visited a friend in Tel Aviv. I left her house late, when buses were running infrequently. Waiting forever at the bus stop, I entertained myself by singing and dancing around. I felt taut with apprehension, anticipating someone inevitably would bother me. At some point, a young man stopped and began talking at me with the usual questions: What are you doing, what are you singing, etc, etc, etc. I can't remember exactly how I responded, but the guy started *yelling* at me. "You're crazy!!! You don't even have a walkman - you don't have any music! You're a lunatic!!!" He was totally in my face.

It is just exhausting.

What was I doing? Living. Breathing. Feeling. Emoting. Enjoying. Seizing the moment while possible. Appreciating being alive. Exploring how much fun I could have in a situation that people usually hate and cannot wait to leave.

What was *he* doing? Feeling entitled to my space and energy, expecting and demanding that I respond to him in an accommodating way - letting him be the master, the point of reference, the one to whom I turn for approval and permission, the MAN. As if by my not giving him a pretty little dress-swishing, eyelash-batting, hair-twirling response, he had the right to assault me.

How to respond? Everything takes energy. Everything. And there is consequence to my self-defense, in a world where this kind of assault is supported. Would people focus on and punish his assault of me or my response to his assault?

Age, Sex, and Power

A few years ago, I was washing off in an open shower on the beach in Herzilleyah. A young teenage boy came over to me, giving me little pickup lines. I was so amazed by the absurdity of the situation that I found it mildly humorous. "Do you want me to soap your back?" he soon asked. "No," I said, unequivocally. He began soaping my back anyhow. Unbelievable. Even boys ten years younger than me feel some sense of power over me and entitlement to my body. "Stop!" I yelled, throwing his arm off me. He apparently was with a group of teenage boys further up the beach, all of whom thought the situation was hilarious.

The boy kept talking at me. He was just a young guy, so I did not feel threatened by him; and so *I did not want to hurt him.* He started soaping me again. I launched into him verbally, and he ran away momentarily, but he and his friends were all laughing. The fact is that he was - and they all were - hurting me. The name of the game is humiliation, power over. And when it is someone in a socially lower power position - namely a boy - doing this power over trip to someone in a socially higher position - a woman - it is especially degrading to the woman and satisfying to the boy.

What would have happened to me if I had beaten the boy up? Would I have been seen as "overreacting?" Would I have been put in jail? Or would I have received support, and if so, from whom - the people on the beach? the police? the store-owners on the beachwalk? Where is the consequence for male violence towards women? If I am the one to dish out that consequence, will there be counter-consequence for *my* actions? And will the consequence for my protecting myself be more than any possible consequence for the guy's initiating assault against me? Who defines the lines and parameters of assault? Who pays the price for these definitions?

Flashback

Two days after my arrival this recent trip, I was waiting in Tel Aviv, for the chartered bus to a conference in Netanya. Having to leave the youth hostel in the morning, I arrived over an hour early at the bus stop. I did not feel like carrying my monstrous backpack around with me everywhere, so I asked some seemingly nice old (male) fabric store-owners if they would mind watching my bag for an hour. They were very pleasant and said it would be no problem.

I returned on schedule to pick up my belongings. The men started asking me questions, doing the small talk thing. They invited me to stay with them for Shabbat, saying they would be like my father to me. Not a great thing to offer, considering the nature of my father's and my relationship; but I understood they meant it in a caring, nurturing way.

After a while, I got ready to leave, and I reached out my hand to shake the hand of one of the old men. He grasped my hand and pulled me towards him for a kiss. I said no. He kept pulling. I said, "NO!" and yanked my hand out of his. Both old men laughed. I wanted to beat up this guy and wreak havoc on his store. 1) But he was old. 2) But "nothing" happened. 3) But the police would side with the old man, for the above reasons. 4) But it would not be *nice*. So I said Shabbat Shalom, still in shock, desperately not wanting this violence, not wanting the situation to be this way...And I cried the whole way to Netanya.

From Here On Out

Embracing the Possibilities

How much better I felt by the end of the trip, after I had begun hitting the men who assaulted me! How good it felt when I defended my space in real, physical, *consequential* ways; how satisfying it was when I turned the tables and took the power in situations where men tried to impose power over me. Through hitting these men, I reclaimed something that was "educated" out of me and most women since birth: the natural, basic commitment to self and to defending one's space.

Pushing the envelope of possible response has given me the power to *choose* whether or not to fight in any given situation - choice being what freedom is all about. With hitting now a concrete option in my repertoire, and no longer just if assaulted *physically*, I sit on the threshold of possibility.

It is from this threshold, where I regularly struggle with the option to hit, that I consciously am aware of how many incentives there are *not* to hit; that I see vividly and feel viscerally how entrenched our system is in supporting male assault of women and enforcing female compliance with this assault. It is from this threshold that I also know the benefits of taking all the risks, breaking all the rules, and claiming my full space in the world; that I poignantly am aware of the deep satisfaction, spiritual transformation, and radiant glee that comes with 100% commitment to defending myself in the face of assault. And it is from this threshold that I see the urgency of providing women with new alternatives and that I see possibilities for doing so.

Through staring the monster in the face - through giving myself additional options, through being willing to consider and act upon that which is taboo - I am *awake:* fully aware of the gains and losses involved in fighting and not fighting; conscious and deliberate about my choice in any given situation. I invite all women to live in this threshold of possibility, by examining what forces encourage and discourage us from fighting at any given time.

Rather than run away from the option out of fear or refuse to consider it out of a blanket dislike of "violence," I call on us to approach the issue with intelligence and wisdom - to identify concretely what forces encourage and discourage hitting, as well as exactly what we gain and lose by hitting or not. If we do not expose the forces motivating our decisions, those forces control us; and if we blindly are controlled, we are not free.

At the very least, stretching our imagination about possibilities will challenge our current notions of how safe we feel, how much violence we tolerate in our daily lives, and what price we pay for our current choices about how to deal with that violence. In discussing possibilities, furthermore, any resistance we may feel to "going that far" may inspire us to come up with alternatives, perhaps more "radical" than how we behave now but less so than hitting.

When I find myself terrified of considering a new possibility in my life, it usually is because I fear discovering that I need to make a drastic change; and I do not want to face whatever pain or chaos that change may cause. By allowing myself just to *consider* a possibility, by allowing myself *not* to act on it, I open myself to honestly evaluating my life. Whatever behavior choice I ultimately make, I act from a place of *consciousness* - knowledge, understanding, and choice - and therefore from a place of power.

What are the implications if we do *not* allow ourselves to examine a possibility for freeing ourselves from violence; if we do not allow ourselves even to *think* about something which perhaps *would* be best for us? Are we not worth evaluating all options for our freedom? Will we give more value to violent men and a misogynistic society; will we be sacrificial lambs in the name of "peace"? If there are options we have not yet explored - ones which just might end the violence against us - are we truly peaceful if we will not even look at them? Or are we in effect conspirators in the violence against us - and are we therefore actually *violent* by *not* considering those options?

What's more, if we do not have the choice of "violence" as an option, is our decision not to be "violent" really peaceful, or is it merely powerless?

I am to my core a gentle soul, the kind of person who sidesteps ants on the street and escorts spiders out of the house. At the drop of a hat, I have and will put myself on the line, risking as much as my life to help other people. Even as a child, I literally put my body between bullies and their victims, preventing several school yard assaults.

Though I never had any question about defending other people, I often had difficulty defending myself. When I was the person targeted for attack, I frequently chose not to fight; because I did "not want to hurt anybody."[24] I reasoned that anyone who needed to lash out must be in tremendous pain; and I did not want to add to that pain. I felt compassion for whoever tried to hurt me, and I held the burden of that person's assault. In this sense, I was quite typically female.

In college, I realized I *was* hurting someone by not fighting: *me.* I realized that *I* am part of the equation, when trying to figure out the least harmful way to respond to a situation. This realization was revolutionary for me at the time, and I feel it is now key on a larger scale, in assessing how to respond to assault against women.

In other words, consider this: *Women count.*

Now consider this: Every one of these women who count is victimized by some form of sexual violence, *every single day.* People who count are being hurt, 24/7. If we truly do not want to participate in hurting people, we by definition must do whatever we can to stop these assaults. Whatever we are doing now clearly *is not enough.* If it were, the violence would be gone already.

If there are ways we can stop violence against women; and we are not engaging in or even willing to look at these possibilities, *then we are complicit in that violence.* It is *because* we hate violence that we must be willing to fight against it. It is *because* we hate violence that we must assess how effective our current forms of resistance against it actually are. It is *because* we hate violence that we must be willing to explore new responses and change our current ones.

What about the option of avoidance, as in flight before fight? The first question I pose is where exactly do we have left to run? The wealthier a woman, of course, the more her options - she can fly or drive to a secluded area.[25] But what about poor women who work several jobs just to get by? They usually do not have access to escape vehicles or time to get away. The second question I pose is, for how long are we willing to contort ourselves around the behavior of men; to alter our own actions out of apprehension for what men might do to us; to make ourselves smaller to avoid men invading our space?

What if we stop contorting ourselves and stop running; what if we become fully present in our bodies and our space; what if we go wherever we want, whenever we want, dressed however we want, and hold men accountable, make *them* pay the price for any attempts to hurt us?

Men overwhelmingly expect and assume - accurately so, in this society - that they can walk through the world without their physical space at constant risk of being invaded. Given the luxury, the *privilege*, of this male reality, men learn to walk through the world with a sense of autonomy, with a sense of *entitlement* to their body space; with a sense of the right to their bodily integrity and the right to physically defend it if threatened.

This sense is reflected, validated, and therefore reinforced all around us in society. It is socially acceptable *and understandable* that men will engage in physical combat if their physical space is threatened. Someone threatening a man's body space - especially in a sexual way - is the aberrant one, is "asking for trouble."

Not so with women. Unlike men, women *cannot* expect and assume that we can walk through the world without our physical space at constant risk of being invaded. To the contrary, women's body space socially is defined as a subset of men's body space. Men have a sense of entitlement not only to their own body space, but to *women's* body space as well. This society does not view as aberrant the men invading women's body space; to the contrary, it views as aberrant the women who *resist*, who defy that invasion. These women threaten the foundation of the patriarchal social order.

IMAGINE if we walked through a world where our bodily integrity was unquestionable and uncompromisable; where we accurately expected and assumed that our physical space would not be invaded; where men perpetrating any degree of violence against us were seen as aberrant; where it was socially acceptable and understandable that we would engage in physical combat if our physical space was threatened; where *we* defined acceptable parameters of behavior and the consequences of overstepping them; where we walked through the world with a sense of autonomy and *entitlement* to our body space; and where this sense was reflected, validated, and therefore reinforced all around us in society...Male privilege. Imagine if we had it.

Imagine if we took it.

Imagine living our lives the way we want, *right now*. Imagine not having to *wait* for the violence against us to end, before we can be as free with our sexuality as we want, with whomever we want; before we can walk in the streets at 1:00 am; before we can wear what we want; before we can say what we want, as loud as we want.

Imagine us no longer having to be careful, but creating a reality where *men* have to be careful. Imagine holding men accountable for their actions, forcing men to face consequences for *their* behavior. Imagine creating a world where violence against women no longer is an option. Imagine women standing up and saying, "You cannot do this to us anymore; *we will not let you.*"

How about if we make ourselves and our emancipation number one. What if we say that men are violent against *us;* that we will protect *ourselves* first; and that if there is a fallout, the men can deal with it, since they created the mess. Men usually are the ones wreaking havoc through their violence, after all, and women usually are the ones scurrying around picking up the pieces.

Only if we refuse to pick up the pieces will men finally have to deal with the fact that our communal "house" is a pigsty because of their violence. Only if we stop being the caretakers will they have reason to start doing some caretaking themselves. The female role of housekeeper is a fundamental part of the patriarchal order. There is no way that by continuing this role we will achieve liberation.

Earlier in this book, I mentioned that by constructing male power on a model of power-*over* women, men inadvertently have placed women at the *center* of their power. As such, the moment women realize and act upon our power in a unilateral way, male dominance over women will be *impossible*, and patriarchy will die.

I believe that men as a group and as individuals know this truth, whether consciously or not. For this reason, they tell us over and over again how weak we are. *If we really were so weak, why would they have to keep pounding this message into our heads?* It is a brainwashing formula for protecting the patriarchal social order, so that women end up conspirators in our own powerlessness. When we realize that we are not weak; when we realize how angry we are about the violence against us; and when we value ourselves enough to take our power and claim our place on this earth, men will be in deep shit.

And they know it.

The Prices We Pay

The question remains how far we are willing to go each day with our fight for liberation - how much we are willing to risk, and in what contexts we are willing to do so. Women's power currently exists in the sense that we *can* stop the dominance; however, it does not exist in the sense of being able to do so without sacrifice. In other words, we have the power to insist on our space, yet we must be prepared for a violent backlash when we do so. A system whose very existence depends on our submission, after all, will fight us to the death to enforce that submission.

If we are going to fight for our freedom, we must be willing to risk as much as our lives. Let us not forget, however, that if we are *not* going to fight for our freedom, we *also* must be willing to risk as much as our lives. What woman, after all, can be certain she will come home alive or even *stay* home alive? The rate of assault against women is staggering.

If we are not going to fight for our freedom, we not only must be willing to risk our *lives,* but must be willing to risk *our souls* as well. If we co-opt to the violence against us, we prevent ourselves from being ALIVE in the greater sense of the word...

In deciding what and when we are and are not willing to fight, we must recognize that regardless of what action or non-action we choose, we *will* pay a price. Once we recognize that there is a price for each action we do or do not take, our choices will be a matter of simple economics, a comparative shopping of activist strategies: getting the most of what we want for the lowest price we can pay.

What price do we pay? I encourage each woman to begin chronicling the various forms of assault that happen to us every day. As we begin writing, we will become aware how often and in how many forms assault actually occurs. We even may resist chronicling the assaults, when we realize how much time it will take to write them all down.

I also encourage each woman to record our physical, emotional, psychological, and spiritual reactions to these assaults. By doing so, we will become conscious of the impact these assaults have on our bodies, our energy, our confidence, our sense of connection, our vibrancy, and so on.

I encourage each of us to chronicle our patterns of avoidance, as well. In other words, how has assault already impacted our lives; how has it intercepted our natural behavior patterns? How has it stood in the way of saying what we think, going where we want, acting how we feel? We may find that actual assaults happen to us minimally but that we circumvent the possibility constantly. We may find that we pacify men before assault can happen[26], by tiptoeing around them or by acquiescing to them whatever they want, before they even can say they want it.

How has the threat of assault cut off our impulses before they could reach the point of consideration or even recognition in our consciousness? Fear surrounding certain behaviors may be so pervasive that the behaviors do not consciously strike us as desirable. Or even as *options*.

For example, I have spoken with women who do not feel this society is violent towards us. "Do you feel safe walking around by yourself in the middle of the night?" I always ask. "Well, I don't go out in the middle of the night," they usually reply. *Viva la* problem! Growing up without certain freedoms presented as options, we may not envision them in our lives at all. Without knowing the world outside the cage, we may not miss it. And so we may not see the bars.

For this reason, as we begin the process of chronicling, we may find ourselves numb. We may feel confused about what constitutes "assault" and what does not. We may not feel the impact assault has on our lives - even if we can identify the assault - because we are so used to it. We may not know how assault has intercepted our authentic behavior patterns. Because we adjusted and reoriented our behavior patterns so long ago, we no longer may know what our authentic patterns are.

Our confusion and numbness themselves will be testament to the profound impact assault has had on our lives: Most of us have been cut off from our instinctual selves. *So start from that place.* It is critical to identify and record exactly where we are in our process, at any given time. Writing about our feelings or lack of feelings is all part of taking inventory. Only once we know where we are and how we got there can we figure out where we want to be and how to get there.

For some women, taking inventory and increasing our consciousness may be enough. For other women, we may want to begin putting our awareness into action. For those of us who want more, I feel the first and most crucial step is to learn self-defense. Unless and until we are able to engage in effective physical combat, we will not have the luxury of saying "no" to men. There is a risk that men physically will attack us when we do not accept whatever form of their violence against us, as a result of the patriarchal system of punishing women who resist. Accordingly, we need to have our bodily resources backing us up and ready to go. When we have the power to back up our words, we have the freedom to say the words we want to say.

Once we have self-defense skills under our proverbial belts, we can begin taking risks, experimenting, pushing the envelopes of responding to assault. We can take baby steps or bold steps: We simply can refuse to smile when he makes that comment, we can hit him, or we can try anything and everything in-between. Or more.

As we begin pushing the envelopes, let us chronicle everything: At what point do we anticipate an assault about to happen? What gives us the clues? How do our bodies feel and react, as the energy shifts? Do we respond to the assault before it happens, or do we wait for it to happen? What motivates our choice of how to behave, and how do we feel about it - before, during, and after? How do people react to the assailant and to us - before, during, and after the assault? How do these reactions change with our different choices of response?

As we explore new behaviors and keep track of our feelings about them, we will act out of a place of ever-growing wisdom, instead of ignorance or apprehension. We may be surprised to find that we like living on the edge, despite whatever risks and fears come with the territory; we may find we like behaving just as we have been; or we may find we like picking and choosing between a wide range of responses, depending on each situation. Whatever behaviors we end up choosing, we will act from a place of knowledge and *choice*, thus from a place of autonomy and power.

Rock the Boat, Baby!

As we get acquainted with and begin to act on our power and potential, we may find that men seem to assault us more frequently; and we may find ourselves suddenly feeling unsafe with men we have trusted. We may react by blaming the assaults on our new behavior and feeling drawn back strongly to our old, familiar ways.

If standing up for and being true to ourselves suddenly "gets" us assaulted, then assault already has been present in and impacted our lives. We simply have not recognized the assault dynamics, because they have been disguised by the thin veil of our complacency. Our self-love, self-respect, and self-embrace cannot *cause* assault. It can, however, unveil the misogyny that lurks dangerously close to the surface of so many male-female interactions.

The question remains whether we want to unveil the misogyny. How much of a commitment do we have to living our authentic lives? How much are we willing to sacrifice ourselves and our power, so as to get by without blatant power clashes? Are we willing to let go of certain comforts we have, so as to make room for a new kind of life? For many of us, our comfort may be the sleep of death: Complacency may come with a feeling of peace, but its price may be our souls.

The fact is that when we embrace and stand up for ourselves, our lives as we know them very well may come crashing to the ground. But consider this: If our full selves cannot exist in our current lives, then hallelujah! Let our current lives come crashing down.

"It is better to die on your feet than to live on your knees." (Dolores Ibarruri)

When I was 21, I knew that I did not want to continue living my life the way I had been living it. I knew the only options were to continue my life "as is" or to jump into an abyss, a complete unknown, where I would risk *absolutely everything* to follow my soul. I literally thought I would die if I jumped into this abyss, but I did it anyway.

My decision came down to one stark moment, when I had the epiphany that there *could be no reconciliation* between the system in which I was living and a healthy life, in which my soul would flourish. The foundations of that system, I realized, stood in direct contradiction to my empowerment. As such, I could not simultaneously hold onto the life I was living and move into a healthy reality. So I left almost everyone and everything I knew.

I then lived through months of excruciating loneliness, deep depression, rage, self-doubt, and fear. I literally could not get out of bed most of the time.

During that period, I met people who helped me on my healing path. Within one and a half years, I emerged on the other side of being a basket case. I became vibrant, healthy, happy, and strong, in ways I never "got" to be before. I became *Me*. I found myself, my path, my voice, the manifestation of the soul that was inside me at birth but squashed out in so many ways.

By letting go of the old life and people, I made room for a new life and new people, ones who nourished my soul. I had no way of knowing things would get better, and none of us ever have any guarantees we will make it. But one thing is certain: Everything will remain exactly the same or get worse, unless we take risks and make changes. And if we embrace ourselves more fiercely with each new challenge, a flower of glorious, vibrant LIFE just might shoot up from the rubble where our old, compromised life dies.[27]

"And the trouble is, if you don't risk anything, you risk even more." (Erica Jong)

I am reminded of the story about my Jewish people during the exodus from slavery in Egypt: When faced with the Red Sea in front of us and the Egyptian soldiers advancing from behind, the masses began yelling at Moses something to the effect of, "Look what you have done! Now we are in worse trouble than we were before! We were better off as slaves in Egypt!"

But were we?

Freedom from slavery unconditionally requires some form of confrontation, and individuals frequently die in the process of fighting for freedom. It is the story behind every revolution. The systems and individuals benefiting from whatever slavery is in place will fight tooth and nail to preserve the social order. They are invested enough in us. The question is, are we invested enough in ourselves?

The only way to get to freedom is to go *forward*, through the proverbial churning sea. Perhaps it will open for us, perhaps it will not. Perhaps we will drown trying to get across; or perhaps as we advance, we will fall into enemy hands and be punished for our attempt to escape. There is no way to know if we will make it through to the other side. But we do know what is behind us, and many of us know that place is intolerable.

"Please know that I am aware of the hazards. I want to do it because I want to do it. Women must try to do things as men have tried. When they fail, their failure must be but a challenge to others." (Amelia Earhart)

Moses never entered the Promised Land, though he led the Jews out of Egypt. We may choose to spend our lives in service to the liberation of women yet never experience the sweet nectar of freedom ourselves. G-d/dess forbid, we may die in the process of fighting. OR we may find that when we rock the foundations of this system, the system opens up and responds in ways we never expected...

Until one is committed
there is hesitancy, the chance to draw back;
ineffectiveness.

Concerning all acts
of initiative and creation,
there is one elementary truth,
the ignorance of which kills countless ideas
and splendid plans:

The moment one definitely commits oneself,
then Providence moves too.
All sorts of things occur to help one
that would never otherwise have occurred.

A whole stream of events issue from the decision,
raising in one's favour
all manner
of unforeseen incidents and assistance,
which no woman could have
dreamt
would have come her way

(adapted from Scottish Himalayan Expedition by WH Murray)

Whatever you can do, or dream you can, begin it.
Boldness has genius, power, and magic in it.

(Goethe)

We each have different circumstances in our lives. Obviously, the more social, economic, or racial privilege we have, the more options we have for living freely; and the less practical struggles we have in embracing that freedom. For example, an "illegal" immigrant woman with children, a physically abusive husband, no job, and no education will face more life-threatening choices and have less resources at her disposal than a wealthy Anglo-Saxon woman with an ivy league education and high-paying job.

Whatever circumstances facing us, let us consider making full use of each and every single resource we *do* have, as well as every bit of energy we have, to move forward towards our liberation. *Let us also make use of whatever privileges we have to help less privileged women move towards their liberation.* And as we experiment with our power and with helping each other, let us beware that there inevitably *will* be a fallout. There will be hard times - and I mean *hard times*, not just "oh, yah, hard times, whatever..." The more we push the envelopes of society, the less society may support us; the less friends we may have; the more people may call us names; the more blatant violence we may face; the less content we may feel; and the more we seriously may question whether we are literally crazy. Sounds appealing, eh?

So why bother rocking the boat? Some of us may choose not to, even after we take honest inventory of our lives and identify how assault impacts us. We may decide that the sacrifices we currently make are better than the sacrifices we will have to make.

So why do *I* bother rocking the boat? Because there can be so much more. Because I see most of us living half-assed, at half-mast, without even knowing it. Because glory is getting squashed, and I am sick of it. Because we each and collectively have so much more power than we utilize. Because if we go all the way, we can overthrow the system. Because I did not come to this planet to live in subservience to someone else's codes. Because my soul wants to burst out in song, dance, and soaring flight, but assholes get in my way constantly. And *that* is not acceptable to me. Period.

"The state of the world today demands that women become less modest and dream/plan/act/risk on a larger scale." (Charlotte Bunch)

When we feel depressed, we may not feel like doing anything to make ourselves happy, *because* we feel depressed. Sometimes we may just have to haul our asses out for a hike, to a movie, or to dinner with a friend, before we even can begin wanting to get out of our funk. We may have to lick a drop of happiness before we can crave it.

On this note, consider taking a leap of faith out of our patterned ways of life, giving ourselves the chance to experience new freedom, before deciding the risks and work that freedom take are not worth it. Consider creating the space for a bigger and better reality to emerge, so that we are not constantly forced to make choices from the limited, constricting framework that exists today.

"You can rest when you're dead." (female athlete in advertisement for sporting gear)

To create a new reality, I believe we must step outside our current mindset and social codes for behavior; for I see no reconciliation between a misogynistic society and woman-loving reality. Our commitment must be to a radical new concept: Women as a point of reference. Women as decision makers, without permission and without apology. Women as powerful individuals who take up space in the physical, spiritual, intellectual, and emotional worlds. Women as a force with whom all of society must contend. Women as a group from whom *others* must ask permission and to whom others must pay upon failing to do so.

Thoughts without the prospect of a home, without a place to land, are sinister to women. We tend to allow ourselves to get involved in a thought only if its logic guarantees it a new resting place. If it does not, if it leads into imponderables, it is quickly pushed away, or not admitted in the first place. " (Christina Thurmer-Rohr)

Since experimenting with hitting men who visually / verbally assaulted me, I have lived in a place that is unclear and uncertain - namely, OK, I did it, I can do it, *now what?* I have struggled with figuring out when to risk and when to hold back; when to take into consideration what might happen and when to say fuck it.

The fact is that within a patriarchal context, commitment to my space and to respectful treatment means *constant fighting*. I am but one individual, and I do not choose to live my life fighting all the time. But I also do not want to let random men violate my space. So I consciously have *avoided* situations as best as possible: I have stayed away from nightclubs, not gone to crowded events, not made eye contact with men as I walked down the street, not been friendly back to friendly men...And when there have been confrontations (because they are impossible to circumvent completely) my primary goal has been to leave rather than to engage.

While writing this book, I have taken a break from my physical process of and experimentation with the issue. I have laid low, to make room for what I see as the next crucial step: gathering support; garnering the troops; creating critical mass; and then going back out into the world again as part of a self-supporting, radical *force* with which society has to contend.

So what will this force look like? What will it do?

Every person who believes in fighting violence against women needs to gather together, pool our resources, and make use of each avenue available to us, to end the insanity. There already are numerous organizations that fight violence against women. We simply need more groups, more people in the groups, more connection and synchronicity between the groups, and additional anti-violence activities for the groups.

Following are my suggestions for what we currently need. Some variations of these groups or practices already may exist - in which case we just need more!

Discussion Groups: *Stories and Strategies*

Apparently, consciousness-raising groups were hot in the sixties. Unfortunately, they do not seem to be around so much anymore. I feel we need to start them up again, with the specific focus of supporting each other in pushing the envelopes of responding to violence. These discussion groups can be a place to swap stories and strategies for fighting verbal, visual, and physical assault: What has worked, what has not, and in what contexts?

These groups also can be a format to discuss and create the following:

Visionary Art: *Creating Alternate Realities*

Kinsey Milhone and VI Warshawski[28] are two feisty, gun-wielding, ass-kicking, mind-speaking, feminist detectives. They may be fictional characters, but they both have impacted my life in very real ways. I always have walked away from the books about them with my spirits lifted, my resolve stronger, and my courage in more abundance. I once went so far as to speak direct quotes from them, when confronting two sexist and otherwise asshole police officers who were mistreating me.

Hothead Paisan is a homicidal lesbian terrorist.[29] Comic strip character though she may be, she validates my anger and fighting spirit, reminds me I am not alone, and...let's just face it: People confuse me with her.

In the past few years, feminist art seems to have proliferated. Either it has grown, or it has gained more exposure; I am not sure. At any rate, we need even more of it: more vision. Each one of us needs to get our creative butts out there and write, sing, paint, or sculpt about the way reality should be. We need to create miniatures of our dream worlds, so that we give each other models of what to strive for. We need to make the food to nourish our battle-weary souls.

Specifically, we need to create images of strong women who kick the shit.

I remember watching the show "Xena the Warrior Princess" a few months ago. The thought, "Yeah, right" went through my head, as I observed women twirling through the air, beating up asshole men. *"Yeah, right"?* Why did that thought not go through my head the zillion times I saw men doing impossible things in movies and on TV? *Because I saw images of men doing those things a zillion times.* Though I always am aware I am watching a movie or TV, the message nonetheless somehow has entered that men can do those ridiculous things, whereas women cannot. Enforce the myth over and over again, and the myth somehow becomes reality.

So we need to create our own myths - and thus our own reality. We need to create and inundate ourselves with images of invincible women: women who fearlessly dish out consequence to assaultive men; women who know without question that we are worth fighting for; women who take on and overthrow whatever stupid systems are in their way. Once we have these images, we just might become these women.

Research: *What Are the Risks? What Are the Methods?*

We need to collect and publish information on exactly what are the risks involved in different behaviors. For example, how dangerous is it *really* for a woman to go out walking at night? How dangerous is it *really* for a woman to hit a man who visually, verbally, or physically assaults her? Does the level of danger vary, according to time or location? How does the danger we face in these situations compare to the danger we face behaving within the confines of the current status quo? How do we define "danger" - what are the risks involved?

How do assailants respond when we hit them? How do law-enforcement officials, people on the street, or store/club/hotel/etc owners respond? Is there a pattern to their responses, or are the responses random?

As part of doing our research, I feel we need to go out in experimental *groups*. For example, let us go to dance clubs in clusters of several women (or women and men). One woman from the group can volunteer as "Madame de Guinea Piggette," dancing by herself. She can try out different responses to different forms of assault; and if any situation gets out of control, her posse can jump into action and protect her. By working in groups, we can take chances and explore behaviors that would be too risky to explore alone.[30]

We also need to do research on what makes some cultures and countries less prone than others to the various forms of sexual assault. For example, why does Denmark seem to have such a relatively low rate of street assault? What is it about that society that creates a more woman-friendly atmosphere? Denmark is one of the most progressive societies today; yet the Danes are descendants of the Vikings, who were extremely violent people notorious for raping women around the globe. How did Denmark transform into the society it is today? How can we transform our society?

Creating Books: *Sharing the Wisdom, Making Connections*

As we individually and collectively experiment with and research pushing the envelopes of female response to male violence, let us create books about our discoveries. I would like to create an anthology, for example, based on the journals of women who take inventory of assault in their lives and experiment with new responses to the assault. By tracking and publishing stories of individual transformation, we can create a stronger culture of female daring.

I also feel we should create a national resource guide for groups that fight violence against women. Perhaps as part of this guide, we should create a comprehensive bibliography of books on the subject.

Training: *Preparing for Battle*

We need to create self-defense programs with a commitment to training women to defend ourselves *as we ourselves define "self-defense."* Currently, there are numerous self-defense groups for women. But how many of these groups would train women, knowing the extent to which we might use the training? In my self-defense classes, women were required to sign a contract that limited our use of the skills we learned. By signing the contract, we effectively were not "permitted" to use our training in ways that could be construed as aggressive.

But what is aggressive? What is defensive? Who is going to decide? And what kind of training are women getting, if we are "permitted" or not "permitted" to use it; if someone else decides for us what kinds of assaults we will resist and how?

When I experimented with hitting men last summer, I specifically did not use techniques I learned in my self-defense training. I was afraid the program would kick me out if news of what I did got back to them. (I still have no idea whether they will continue to train me, once this book is available...)

If women are going to experiment with responses to assault; if we are going to push the envelopes of our behavior, we need to be prepared to go all the way in defending ourselves. As I have mentioned before, we should expect a violent backlash to our newfound power. We *must* be prepared for it, and our self-defense schools must support us in confronting it. For this reason, women who already are trained and who are committed to revolutionary self-defense need to bond together and create places to train the women who will fight for us all on the front lines. And I believe this training should include everything from how to yell, "No!" to how to carry and shoot semi-automatic weapons.

Community Patrol Groups: *Taking to the Streets*

Once we are trained, I feel we need to create community patrol groups to protect each other - to intervene in domestic violence, to escort women through high-crime areas, and to prevent the various forms of street assault.

Should these patrol groups carry guns? I think the more protection, the better. Since extreme, life-threatening situations may arise, I do feel community patrol groups should be armed. I know women generally have an intense dislike of guns; but if forced to choose between protecting ourselves or not carrying guns, should we not choose protecting ourselves?

These patrol groups also should be responsible for alerting neighborhoods to the existence of known rapists or wife-beaters. The groups can use guerrilla tactics that already have been explored, such as wheat-pasting posters that show the men's faces and have statements such as, "This man is a rapist. He lives at [insert address]."

Underground Railways: *Creating Safe Space*
I recently saw a video about women with life sentences in prison for killing their batterers. Though it did not surprise me that these women were sentenced, I was shocked to find out that half of the women interviewed had killed their batterers *while their batters were trying to kill them.* Wo. Scary shit. That is intense patriarchy in action.

As I mentioned earlier in the book, the current legal "justice" system is not protecting us; moreover, it is punishing us for protecting ourselves. We need to create safe spaces for women to go so that we have the option of defending ourselves without being punished.

Can we live on the run forever? What should be the extent of these underground railways? To bust a woman out of her home or out of jail? To take a woman out of a state or out of the country? To arrange for her to get a whole new set of identification papers? To get her cosmetic surgery and hair coloring, so as to completely alter her appearance? How can we accomplish these things?

For anyone who ever questioned why more Europeans did not hide Nazi prey, here is your chance to prove you would have done differently. We need to think seriously and act subversively, and we need to do it now.

Legal Networks: *The System on Our Side*
The Suffragettes landed in jail numerous times, and all they wanted was to vote. We need to think ahead and create a serious legal network for ourselves: We need lawyers who believe in women hitting men who visually/verbally assault and lawyers who believe in women killing men who physically assault - whether as a preventive life-saving measure or in the moment of fighting for life. We need quick-witted lawyers with a mind for working every possible loophole and a drive for winning every case. We need activists who can make the law work for us.

Guerrilla groups: *Prevention through Fear*
Terror of rape seems to be what keeps women immobilized, more than actual rape itself. Perhaps if men feared women's retaliation against rape, they would think twice before raping. In other words, perhaps we can introduce the terror factor to men.

I know nothing about girl gangs, and I am extremely curious about them. Do they operate from a place of feminist consciousness? Can they serve as a model for the creation of women's guerrilla groups?

What would women's guerrilla groups look like and do? Here are some ideas: When a man rapes a woman and 1) is not charged, 2) is let off on a technicality, or 3) is given a short sentence, a secret group of women will go and 1) beat up, 2) castrate, or 3) kill the rapist once he returns home. They will leave a note with some group logo, saying this retaliation will continue to happen until rape stops. Press will be tipped off, so the event will get high publicity (remember the press coverage Lorena Bobbit got).

Rapists targeted will be chosen in deliberately different states, to make the guerrilla activity seem as widespread and random as possible. The activity will be repeated only a few times, until the country is in a complete tizzy.

How will women know who to trust to join such a group?[31] What will be specific strategies to avoid arrest? What will be specific strategies for handling the press, so the publicity will work to the benefit of anti-rape work? Current "radical" feminist groups, after all, will look like pussycats in comparison. How will mainstream feminist groups be approached - or will anyone bother approaching them?

Writing about the possibility of guerrilla groups is scary. How do I know the FBI will not come and nab me just for writing about them? (Has w'halila) I do not want to organize or take part in a guerrilla group - too much for me to risk in this lifetime - but I do want to put the idea out there, in case it appeals to anyone else. Maybe old women who suffered at the hands of patriarchy their whole lives would like do it as a final thrill on this planet???

Women Up in Arms

Three years ago, I began writing something called "Women Up in Arms." I had to stop shortly after I started; because it was so intense for me that I started getting sick and everything started looking yellow, from a burning sensation. Two years ago, I picked it up and started writing again. And again, everything started looking yellow, and I had to stop. Last year, I hit several men. I felt great. And suddenly, the words I had been wanting to say found their way onto the page.

This book is about expanding women's options for protecting our space. It is about asserting that we have the *right* to protect our space, right down to the last "hey baby" or eyeball on our breasts. It is about heightening our consciousness, becoming aware of what price we pay each day that we just try to get by. It is about asserting that we have more power and possibility than we think and that living from that place of power and possibility not only is legitimate but also is *fun*.

For those who still maintain that they do not want to participate in any form of physical combat whatsoever, I tip my hat to you and challenge you to come up with alternatives. Hurrah if there is another way we can stop this insanity. I do not want to yell, hit, shoot, or even say mean words to anyone. But I guarantee that I will do any and all of the above if I must to protect my space.

For those who are not staunch pacifists yet still feel queasy from my writing, I ask the following: Do you support the United States or another country having an army? Let me remind you that the United States did not start off with an established, world-approved military. To the contrary, it started off with a bunch of wild-eyed rebels spouting crazy notions of freedom and equality, hiding in trees and shooting at Brits.[32] Would you have approved of their resistance if you had lived at that time?

Having an army is about protecting one's space. Are we not just as entitled as the United States to protecting our own space? Are we not even more entitled? Especially considering that this republic does not protect our space as women, why hand it the authority to dictate the parameters of our behavior?

And some basic points: Big fish eat little fish. Predators prefer easy prey. Schoolyard bullies pick on kids who do not fight back. What more, those bullies STOP picking on those kids when those kids finally DO fight back. Why do men target women for attack several hundred percent more times than they target men for attack? Because women usually take shit. Men usually fight.

So we do not like war. Well, the war against women rages on, whether or not we fight. Are we going to sit back and let it eat us alive? Think of it visually: Every time a man assaults a woman, it is as if a bomb drops on another piece of land. Will we run from area to area, trying to escape the never-ending barrage? Or will we destroy the source of those bombs before those bombs destroy us?

Is my thinking male thinking? *Have we been so brainwashed to think that the basic instinct for and commitment to self-protection is male?* Male thinking actually is the notion that I as a woman will not and should not have the desire or ability to defend myself and my space. What a convenient formula for domination. *Who does it serve?* Not I.

The May/June 1994 issue of Ms. Magazine was from front to back an anti-women-carrying-guns issue. Several women wrote letters to the editor in response. I would like to share some of what these women said:

Kimberly: "Two years ago, in my junior year in college, I was stalked by a former friend. This man's behavior became increasingly bizarre - following me around, leaving threatening notes, calling me constantly, and throwing rocks at my window in the middle of the night, in an attempt to lure me outside. I felt like a hunted animal. I filed a report with the campus police and the next time he showed up, they kicked him off campus. Soon after, I moved into my own apartment. I gave my new phone number to maybe three friends with strict instructions to keep it secret. Unfortunately, two weeks later he tracked down one of these friends at one in the morning and intimidated him into releasing my phone number. From 1:00 am to 7:00 am, I received 35 death threats on my answering machine. I called the police, who arrived in time to answer the thirty-sixth call. The police managed to scare him away, and I filled out all the official papers to have him kept away from me, but I still live in fear of him. The police may not be able to help next time.

"I have moved away from where he lives, but I still must go to the city occasionally. Each time I do, I am vigilant. But I carry a handgun, because I don't want to risk his actually trying to kill me. If he ever comes near me, I will kill him. I don't see a problem with this, unlike Jones and Neuborne [who wrote anti-gun articles in the issue], who feel that they are abandoning the moral high ground if they even own a gun.

"Do you really think that women are going to be safer if men like this are subjected to no more than consciousness-raising sessions? Do you really believe that the ex-boyfriends and ex-husbands responsible for the murders of women could be stopped by a stern talking-to? Give me a break! Women have to be realistic about protecting themselves while working for victims' rights, medical coverage for battered women, more shelters for abused women, and less brutality. [italics added]

"Women's safety is a key women's issue and a right. The National Rifle Association is doing something practical and realistic about solving women's safety problems. You have yet to come up with something better."

Minerva: "Your issue on guns was a disservice to both women and feminism. Your articles ignored the overwhelming data in favor of women protecting themselves with firearms...

"The reason that the media never publicize the proper use of guns for self-defense is because such stories don't sell papers. How do I know this? Four years ago I shot and wounded a man who was breaking into my apartment. He had a record for rape and burglary. The press never did a story on my experience. If guns had been illegal, as you desire, I would be dead or raped (or both)...

"Until the government can guarantee my safety, I have the right to defend myself effectively! If someone tries to grab me as I walk from work to my car, he's going to get hot lead in his gut. *Yes, I am an empowered feminist.*"

Adriene: "Jones [in her anti-gun article] bases her argument on...reminders of women's famed concern for society's 'general welfare.' Only briefly is the story of one woman described: April LaSalata, threatened by her murderous ex-husband, applied for, but was denied, a permit to carry a gun. LaSalata was then attacked and killed by the man she feared....Jones treats the question of LaSalata's life as a minor one. [Jones'] point is that she does not want to live in a world where she must own a gun. Jones is alive and April LaSalata, who wanted to live, is not.

"It is ironic that [in] this same issue, Ms gave the armed women of the Zapatista Army of National Liberation unqualified respect and support...Ms. apparently finds no need for an anti-gun stance when a worthy uprising is sanctioned and led by men. [italics added] I love Ms., but I wish you had dealt more honestly, courageously, and consistently with the subject of guns, the complexities of personal self-defense, and the need to stop men's ongoing war against women."

Martha: "Embracing women's capacity for violence will not feed male violence mania but, rather, *take the fun out of violence* for men and change things in ways we cannot yet imagine."[33]

Passive Vs. Peaceful

A few months ago, a guy at my YMCA gym harassed me in a disgusting way. Recently, I saw him again in the weight room. I wanted to get his name, to report him to the management. I asked the staff in the weight room if he knew the guy's name. The staff did not want to get involved: "I'm a peaceful person," he said.

Really?

Then why not hold the man accountable for harassing a woman? Why not help me find out this guy's name and get his membership suspended? Why not help me teach this guy harassment is not acceptable? Why not help me prevent this guy from harassing other women in the gym? Non-action *is* action. Passivity endorses violence by not resisting it.

My Knight in Shining Armor

In high school, my favorite book was *The Sea Wolf,* the story of a man's journey out to sea. You know, your basic testosterone I'm-gonna-transform-into-a-real-man type Odyssey journey.

I loved it.

And why not? Why not have our own transformational journeys, where we face unbeatable odds and beat them anyway? Why not go into the heart of the ocean, the forest, the desert...or the patriarchy, face our greatest fears, our greatest obstacles, our greatest challenges, and come out on the other side *vibrantly alive,* self-assured, and all the wiser?

I strongly believe that women need to go on our own expeditions into the unknown, dangerous world. We need to be our own warriors, our own defenders, our own princes, our own knights in shining armor. True, there are no guarantees. Risk comes with daring. But so does exhilaration, freedom, and connection with the life force that pulses through us. And is that not what life is all about?

Notes

1. "Mizrahi" describes the Jewish people and heritage indigenous to the Middle East and North Africa. "Ashkenazi" describes the Jewish people and heritage from Eastern Europe, Germany, and Austria.

2. "Power" - as in political power; not self-power, not true power

3. In addition, of course, to other complex reasons. This dynamic is just one of the many that play out.

4. Not positive in the true sense of the word; rather "positive" in the male lens sense of women being receptive, compliant, non-confrontational.

5. For the purpose of this book, I refer to heterosexual male identity. It of course is important to consider how sexual identity and sexual politics shape and change this construct, but it is beyond the scope of my work at this time.

6. I do not equate being a little boy with being a coward, and I am conscious of the ageism and sexism inherent in that statement. Though I do not actually agree at all with the statement, I made it so as to speak in a "language" that would have impact on these jerks. My goal was to fight the battle and get the desired response.

7. Even in cases of extreme physical attack, most male violence against women seems to go unpunished. For example, marital rape is still legal in many US states. What's more, many women have been jailed for killing assailants *while* the assailants attempted to kill the women.

8. See footnote 7.

9. See footnote 7.

10. The irony is that I actually came to Eilat to take a break from the verbal/visual assault I had been encountering in Tel Aviv.

11. I acknowledge that this dynamic happens with women as well, whether in lesbian or straight relationships. My understanding is that it does not happen anywhere near as frequently as with men, especially in the context of heterosexual relationships. I also acknowledge that this dynamic happens between two men. Again, for this book, I am addressing male-female patterns of interaction and in that context, male violence towards women.

12. It is not acceptable to have to choose between being sexual/being violated and not being sexual/not being violated. Violence should not happen, period, especially in the context of intimacy. It is a

loaded (though common) question to ask if a woman should have stopped being intimate with a man, putting the burden of his behavior on her shoulders. My choice was to keep going, trusting that Gil was my partner at the time, and not wanting to have to stop being sexual with him; because what should have stopped was *his* violence.

13.   Even then, my hitting him might not be considered self-defense (see footnote #7). For hitting to be considered self-defense, there must be a certain amount of weakness involved on the part of the woman - namely, not stopping violence from escalating to the point where it is legal for her to begin hitting. If women stop violence at the point where energy *begins* to shift - and *we know* where it is going - then neither law nor general society treat us as having fought in self-defense. Only if we let violence run its course are we supported in fighting - and by that time, violence is exponentially more difficult to fight, if not too late. I find that our society's philosophy on "self-defense" is similar to the philosophy currently behind insurance company "health" policies: Companies will cover the costs of an operation but not of preventive health measures such as yoga or acupressure. In both cases, I find the philosophy to be foolish and destructive.

14.   Perhaps part of the resistance from society is an ingrained belief that a sexual woman is not an innocent woman, that a sexual woman deserves to be punished for her sexuality. I feel it is for this reason that the media gets outraged at the rape of an elderly "lady" or pre-pubescent girl but not at the rape a woman who falls in between these "non-sexual" ages (an issue in itself - of course older women have sex drives). Women are put in a life-threatening catch 22: Men sexualize us regardless, then society treats us as "sluts" who deserve violence because we are sexual.

15.   Seven Year Bitch, "M.I.A.," in ¡*Viva Zapata!* (C/Z Records, 1407 Madison #41, Seattle, WA 98122)

16.   Shbu'oth: Jewish holiday celebrating G-d's giving the Torah (Jewish Bible) to the Jewish people, as we wandered in the desert between Egypt and the Promised Land.

17.   Shouk: Middle Eastern/North African marketplace, similar to a flea market in the States.

18.   I wonder how much wanting Gil to know *why* I was hitting him was a manifestation of my learned caretaking impulse - why not just HIT HIM? *I* would know why. Would that be enough or not? I still feel ambivalent.

19.   I want to emphasize that I specifically am referring to *street* harassment. I have experienced and witnessed religious men getting in women's space, big time; however I have found it happening predominantly in relationship contexts. Let it be said for the record that religious men molest and rape women, as do men from any other background. My sense, however, is that it happens mostly in the

context of domestic abuse. I wonder if any studies have been done on the means and extent of sexual violence within this community.

20.   Kotel: Western Wall, the holiest site in the Jewish religion. It is the last remaining wall of the Temple from ancient Israel, destroyed first by the Babylonian empire and last by the Roman empire.

21.   Shabbat Shalom: "peaceful Sabbath," the greeting people say to each other on the Jewish Sabbath, which starts Friday night at sundown and ends Saturday night at sunset (25 hours long).

22.   24 hours a day, 7 days a week

23.   I would not expect such support from a man or an older person, and he was both. What more, he was from my community of people, so I felt supported from *within*. Lastly, his support yet again countered the popular notion that Mizrahi men are more sexist than Ashkenazi men. My experience time and again has been to the contrary. Shimon from the Eilat Youth Hostel, parenthetically, also was Mizrahi.

24.   As I recall, my non-resistance was almost exclusively in the context of verbal abuse. A few girls used to harass me constantly and may have jumped me once, but boys never touched me. Throughout my school years, boys were afraid of me, positive I would beat them up successfully if I felt like it. In middle school, two boys in particular used to molest all the girls. I was about the only one they did not touch. I made it clear I would bash their heads in if they even thought about it.

25.   Of course, secluded areas do not necessarily feel safe to many women. Because I am trained in self-defense, I prefer secluded areas, where I escape the constant street assault and reconnect with nature.

26.   Although assault may happen anyway; the "rules" are arbitrary and not necessarily followed by the men.

27.   The following activities have helped me "flower": Actively questioning my thoughts and behaviors; keeping a regular journal; making music and art; practicing yoga; participating in activist groups; taking self-defense; becoming athletic; regularly visiting the ocean and mountains; and attending healing-oriented workshops and meetings.

28.   VI Warshawski is the lead character in Sarah Paretsky's murder mysteries, and Kinsey Milhone is the lead character is in Sue Grafton's. Both series are commonly available in bookstores and public libraries.

29.   Hothead Paisan comics are created and published by Diane DiMassa, c/o Giant Ass Publishing, PO Box 214, New Haven, CT 06502. Available in feminist bookstores.

30.   I attribute this idea to my friend Dorothy.

31.   Melanie Kaye/Kantrowitz mentions this concern in "Women and Resistance," in *The Issue is Power* (Aunt Lute Books)

32.   I specifically am referring to the rebels in the context of their relationship to the British. Obviously, these same individuals and their descendants were racist, Jew-hating, and sexist and did great harm to native Americans and all other non-Christian, non-White, non-male people on this land.

33.   *Ms.* Magazine, August/September 1994, Letters to the Editor